The Lost Colony

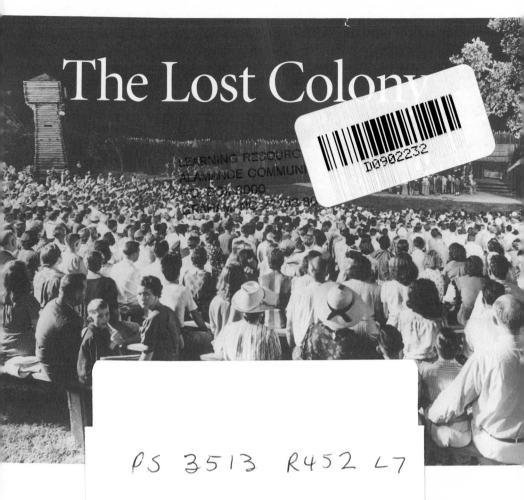

PS 3513 R452 L7

DK

GAYLORD FG

Edited, with an Introduction and a Note on the Text, by

LAURENCE G. AVERY

The University of North Carolina Press Chapel Hill and London

Lost Colony

A SYMPHONIC DRAMA OF AMERICAN HISTORY

by Paul Green

Set in Minion by Eric M. Brooks

Manufactured in the United States of America

The paper in this book meets the guidelines for

permanence and durability of the Committee on

Production Guidelines for Book Longevity of the

Council on Library Resources.

Library of Congress

Cataloging-in-Publication Data

Green, Paul, 1894–1981.

The Lost Colony: a symphonic drama of

American history / by Paul Green; edited,

with an introduction and a note on the text,

by Laurence G. Avery.

    p. cm.

"A Chapel Hill book."

ISBN 0-8078-4970-7 (alk. paper)

1. Roanoke Colony—Drama.   2. Roanoke Island

(N.C.)—Drama.   I. Title.

PS3513.R452 L7   2001

812'.52—dc21   2001025339

05 04 03 02 01   5 4 3 2 1

CONTENTS

ILLUSTRATIONS

1937–1939 (following page 44)
Site where Waterside Theatre was later built
Ben Dixon MacNeill and Paul Green inspect unfinished stage of
  Waterside Theatre
Waterside Theatre in its first season
Paul Green discusses *The Lost Colony* with actors
Audience watching Reverend Martin baptize the infant Virginia Dare
President Franklin Roosevelt, with Governor Clyde Hoey and
  Congressman Lindsay Warren, at *The Lost Colony*
Eleanor Roosevelt, with Paul Green and D. B. Fearing,
  at *The Lost Colony*

Late 1940s–1970s (following page 72)
Waterside Theatre about 1950
The Historian in his fancier booth after World War II
Uppowoc mourning the death of King Wingina
John Borden rallies the colonists before departure at Plymouth
Women mending fishing net on Roanoke Island
Agona offers to relieve Old Tom of his load
Father Martin christens the infant Virginia Dare
John Borden and Eleanor Dare at the death of Captain Ananias Dare
Old Tom on guard

1998–2000 (following page 108)
Waterside Theatre after the 1997–98 renovation
Prologue, with cast ranged across the stage
Sir Walter Raleigh presents Wanchese and Manteo to Queen Elizabeth
Challenged by Manteo, Wanchese demands that the English colonists
  leave Roanoke Island
Agona offers to relieve Old Tom of his load
Sir Walter Raleigh pleads with Queen Elizabeth to allow aid for the
  Roanoke colony
The colonists leave Fort Raleigh on their final march

INTRODUCTION: At *The Lost Colony*

At *The Lost Colony*, performed outdoors during the summer on coastal Roanoke Island, weather matters. The weather does not always cooperate. Occasionally it rains. Sometimes it is hot and sticky. Every few years a hurricane blows through. But usually by 8:30, when performances start, the weather is tolerable. Once in a while it is perfect.

July 20, 2000, was one of those happy evenings. The morning had been overcast, but a breeze in the afternoon cleared the sky and the temperature rose to 77°. Around 8:00, when people began finding their seats in the Waterside Theatre, the temperature was 75° (and would drop to 70° before the show ended at 10:50). Many people came in from the beaches in shorts but with pullover sweaters or windbreakers tied around their waists. The man next to me, from Long Island, was at Nags Head for the week with his wife, seated on the other side of him. She was the member of the family who wanted to see *The Lost Colony*. He declared himself more at home in Broadway theaters. I watched the first stars appear while dusk still held enough light to outline the stage against Roanoke Sound. In the row behind me a little girl, maybe four and wearing a yellow dress, climbed into her mother's lap and wondered when the play would begin.

The Lost Colony began in 1937. That was the 350th anniversary of the earliest attempted English settlement in North America, on Roanoke Island in 1587, and people in eastern North Carolina had long been frustrated by what seemed to them the neglect of that important event by historians and in the popular mind. Knowing the religious pageant at Oberammergau, Germany, they thought of staging a pageant themselves to raise awareness of the colony (the anniversary would provide a needed rallying point) and turned to Paul Green to write it. Green, who had won a Pulitzer Prize in 1927 for the first of his several Broadway plays, was a natural for the job. Steeped in North Carolina history and lore, he had in fact dreamed of writing a play about the Roanoke colonists since his college days in the early 1920s.

Everyone associated with the project knew it was a long shot. (The sponsoring organization, the Roanoke Island Historical Association, led by W. O.

1

Saunders, editor of the Elizabeth City *Independent*, and D. B. Fearing, wholesale grocer in Manteo and a state senator from Dare County, was hesitant at first about assuming financial responsibility for the production.) The question was, would people come to see the show? That is a worry anytime you put on a play, but it had real urgency when the play was on Roanoke Island. It wasn't because the area was densely populated that the Wright brothers had gone to nearby Kitty Hawk some years earlier to test their flying machines. Towns in the region were scarce (the makeup of Dare County suggests why: 300 square miles of land, 1,200 square miles of water). None of the towns at the time had a population of more than 10,000. Manteo, on Roanoke Island, its streets paved with shells, was closest to the site of the colony and the play, and home to 547 people. About twice that many lived in Wanchese, a fishing village and the other town on the island.

So, for the play to prosper, people would have to come from far away (relatively speaking). The trouble was, there was no good way to get there. A contemporary document, *North Carolina: A Guide to the Old North State*, compiled by the Federal Writers' Project of the Work Projects Administration (WPA) and published in 1939, gives details of life at the time. The route onto Roanoke Island from the north involved a ferry ride (seventy-five cents for car and driver, ten cents for each additional passenger), a stretch on something called "the floating road" (at the time—it had taken several forms over the years—a sixteen-foot-wide strip of asphalt suspended on steel cables hitched to pilings over several miles of swamp that would swallow up anything falling into it), the rest of the way on roads that were little more than packed sand. The other and easier approach to the island, from the west, consisted of miles of sandy dirt roads and two toll ferries, one across the Alligator River (so named because alligators frequented the water there), the other from Manns Harbor, jumping-off place on the mainland, a crossing of Croatan Sound that took thirty minutes. (The ferry made a round-trip every hour and a half between 7:30 A.M. and 6:30 P.M., so you might wait a while at Manns Harbor before departing for the island.)

Despite all of which, Fearing, Saunders, Green, and the rest went merrily on. A large contingent of so-called CCC boys was already encamped on Roanoke Island (men in the Civilian Conservation Corps, a forerunner of the WPA, who were building up sand dunes on the outer banks in one of the early futile efforts to stabilize those barrier islands), and Fearing got a crew of them, with mules and scoops, to work on the theater, grading the seating area and building up a stage at water's edge. Theater equipment came from the Rockefeller Foundation (an organ for musical accompaniment) and the

University of North Carolina in Chapel Hill (lights and related gear). The university also supplied the director (Samuel Selden) and several actors (numerous local residents also acted in the play, as did men from the CCC camp). Actors for the leading parts were professionals provided by the Federal Theatre Project. The U.S. Postal Department issued a Virginia Dare stamp to publicize the event, and the Treasury minted a Dare/Raleigh half-dollar, allowing the Roanoke Island Historical Association to sell the coins for $1.50 apiece to raise money.

The Lost Colony was a child of its era. At no other time could it have been gotten together in just the way it was in 1937. With its grassroots origin, community spirit, and celebratory aim, the production was precisely the sort of effort to attract national attention during the New Deal phase of the Great Depression. Paul Green recalls those early days in two essays included at the end of the present edition. The play opened on July 4 (a Sunday) with about 2,500 people in attendance, then played Friday, Saturday, and Sunday nights through Labor Day. A leading drama critic, Brooks Atkinson of the New York Times, gave the play an enthusiastic review during the season. President Roosevelt attended a performance on August 18, birthday of Virginia Dare, first child of English parents born in America, and the play became a cause for Eleanor Roosevelt in her efforts to enrich the lives of depression era Americans through the arts. Exact attendance figures do not exist, since record keeping was not a strong point that first season, but people managed to get there. The best estimates are that the play had an audience of about 50,000 during the summer of 1937.

The performance I saw in 2000 differed in a number of ways from the performance people saw in 1937. The four-year-old behind me that July night pinpointed one of the elements that had changed over time. In the 2000 season the show opened with the whole cast on stage, engaged in choral speaking, some lines delivered by individuals, some by small groups, key words and phrases echoed for emphasis across the stage. Even with clear articulation and good timing, which the cast displayed, such speaking wants careful listening, and the little girl, attentive only at intervals during the evening, asked her mother in more than a stage whisper: "What are they saying?" Behind the question is the history of the narrator in the play, a kind of character always full of problems in the theater.

The narrator in The Lost Colony, called the Historian, is a natural response to the demands of the play. While The Lost Colony is a play rather than a pageant in the sense that it has well-developed characters and a plot governed by its theme, not by the sequence of historical events, it is nevertheless a historical play and episodic in structure. The action transpires over a period of four to five years, 1584 to 1588, sometimes in England, sometimes on Roanoke Island, and audiences need to understand the historical situation behind the action, particularly the rivalry between England and Spain in Renaissance Europe. A narrator is an efficient vehicle for introducing historical background and for bridging the gap between episodes a few months or years or an ocean apart.

The trouble with narrators is that they are not part of the action of the play but outside it. When they speak, they interrupt dramatic momentum, disrupt any sense audiences have of being caught up in the ongoing action. So narrators tend to be a drag on performance. The history of this useful but troublesome kind of character in *The Lost Colony* is a story of attempts over the years to hold onto the benefits of a narrator but to minimize the character's disruptive impact. The story so far has three chapters.

Production photographs and stage directions in the first edition of the play show that in 1937 the Historian's psychic separation from the action was paralleled by a physical separation as well. What audiences saw in 1937 was "a sort of niche or alcove built into the bank at the immediate left front of the proscenium. Here as if seen through a transparent gauze is a group of fifteen or twenty men and women who constitute the commenting and interpretive chorus throughout the play. They are dressed in gray smock-like vestments. Down in the middle forefront of them and seated at a little table with a light and a great open book is the elderly historian and chorus leader who is also dressed like the chorus. He begins reading aloud . . . 'In the time of Queen Elizabeth . . .'" (1937, p. 6). For several decades nothing essential changed in the situation of the Historian. The supporting group disappeared (as did two other narratorlike characters), leaving the Historian as the sole narrative voice in the play, and his alcove (literally a three-sided cubicle open toward the audience), at first roofless and rustic, grew grander over the years. But in grandeur or not, there he sat at his table to the left of the stage as audiences view it, reading from his book, his aloofness from the dramatic action signaled unmistakably by his isolation in the cubicle.

The first consequential change in the deployment of the Historian occurred in the mid-1960s, when the cubicle was done away with and the Historian became mobile. Stage directions in a text from 1980 suggest what audiences saw during those years: "(light) comes up at the front of the center stage to disclose the historian of the occasion who stands illuminated in a circle of light. He is a kindly, elderly man, dressed in a scholar's dark robe and carries a ledger book. . . . He opens his book, glances at it and closes it. Addressing the audience: 'In the time of Queen Elizabeth the First . . .'" (1980, pp. 1–3). This is the way the Historian was handled for about three decades. Some years his costume was the scholar's robe, other years he wore Elizabethan garb or modern dress clothes. Usually, I think, he did not carry a book and addressed the audience with no pretense of reading. Whatever his costume and props, he delivered his lines from the sloping front of the stage (center, left, or right). This put him in the sight lines from audience to stage so that visually, at least, he seemed more nearly involved in the action of the play than when he was off in a side-stage cubicle.

The choral speaking of the 2000 season was introduced the season before. The basic step was to cut the Historian as a character and distribute all of his lines to characters involved in the dramatic action. Distribution was done with sensitivity to the nature of the characters. Lines having to do with the life of Native Americans, for instance, are taken by Wanchese and Manteo, principals among the Native American characters. Lines having to do with the dream of an English settlement in the New World are taken by Sir Walter Raleigh and his associates. And so forth. The lines beginning "In the time of Queen Elizabeth the First" are spoken by the Queen herself. At the opening of the play characters are disposed from one side of the stage to the other, more prominent characters occupying center stage. During the course of the play, when characters deliver lines from the Historian's speeches, they signal that they are momentarily moving beyond their own character by some physical orientation, such as walking briskly away from another character and speaking, as if delivering a soliloquy, at an angle to the audience.

These changes over time in the handling of the Historian show the impact of artistic directors on yearly productions. Joe Layton, a Broadway choreographer, began a long tenure as director of the play in 1964 and was responsible for moving the Historian from his side-stage cubicle to the forestage between the audience and the action. Drew Scott Harris, an experienced director in the current professional theater, was artistic director of *The Lost Colony* for the seasons of 1998, 1999, and 2000, and in 1999 introduced the choral speaking format.

The man from Long Island next to me at the July 2000 performance was better disposed toward the play at intermission than at the outset, when it seemed he had come only to placate his wife. His comment at intermission was that he had "always wondered what those Greek plays were like on stage, with their chorus and all, and now I have a sense of it." I remembered the comment when I looked back at the stage direction about the Historian in the 1937 edition, where he was thought of as the leader of a fifteen- or twenty-person group "who constitute the commenting and interpretive chorus throughout the play." Clearly, as he imagined his own play, Paul Green was thinking of those great tragedies from early Athens and how they were staged. However the Historian and his chorus were handled in the first seasons of *The Lost Colony*, the introduction of choral speaking in 1999 was a move in the direction of the original conception rather than away from it. In performance the choral speaking also softened the sense of suspension in the action, and of momentum lost, when the Historian's lines are delivered.

Other changes since 1937 are numerous, some made primarily to control the running-time of performances. Any production concerns itself with running-time because people can sit still only so long, but for a play done outside with a sizable number of family groups in the audience, limiting factors accumulate. Beth Stewart, associated with *The Lost Colony* for several years and in 2000 its production manager, told me they could not start before 8:30 without losing the effect of stage lights because of too much light still in the evening sky. And they felt they had to let out by 11:00 at the latest so families could get the children home and to bed. (In 2000, act 1 ran fifty-four to fifty-five minutes, act 2 sixty-one to sixty-two minutes. Starting between 8:30 and 8:35 and with a twenty-minute intermission, typically the play was over between 10:45 and 10:55.)

In the theater it rarely happens that scripts are too short, so control of running-time means cutting things. An example of things cut from the acting script of *The Lost Colony* consists of biblical allusions and folk sayings that enliven the language of Old Tom, an important comic character in the play. These sayings and allusions have been cut from the production script over the years mainly in the interest of moving the action along. Another example is the brief encounter between Sir Walter Raleigh and William Shakespeare in act 1, scene 4. The episode has been used in performance only rarely since the 1950s. A few moments of individual suffering among the colonists have also been eliminated in the final scene of the play.

The other basic reason for changes in the play over the years is that audiences change. The world today is a different place from the depression world of the 1930s. While core values may remain viable (in *The Lost Colony* they are love in various human relationships, courage, and an egalitarian social order), audiences bring changing experiences and expectations to the play every summer. Artistic directors can't look on the play as a museum piece, as a memorial to something grand in the past. They must deal with audiences in the here and now and make the play a moving experience for the audience that night. The Indians in the play—or indigenous people, or Native Americans—show how changing social attitudes can affect the play.

In 1937 *The Lost Colony* was probably ahead of most of its audience in the way it conceived the Algonquian people who greeted the first English settlers in North America. While the play accepted the historical fact of European claims of sovereignty over New World territory, it did so not without irony. The first view of the Algonquians in the play is during a harvest festival in which an elaborate dance-pantomime reaches a climax with the promise of an abundant harvest and happy future. Immediately, however, the festival is interrupted by the arrival of the English ("Somewhere in the distance the long brazen note of an English horn is suddenly blown" [1937, p. 11]), and the Algonquians are left stunned and fearful, no longer knowing what the future holds. Later texts show the Historian commenting on the pantomime and making the irony explicit (he may have commented in the first years too, without the text showing it, since it is difficult to convey precise information in pantomime). After noting that the god of the Algonquians seems pleased with their worship and promises a bountiful harvest, the Historian ominously adds: but their god "deceived them. Instead of plenteous crops and bounteous fish from the waters for the year ahead, these trusting people receive the Englishman" (1980, p. 6). A few scenes later the play makes clear the cost to the Algonquians of the English intrusion when it shows an English commander brutally slaughtering the Algonquian chief and most of his retinue.

The play also shows a romance and the makings of a marriage between an English man and Algonquian woman, the comic Old Tom and sometimes comic Agona. "That was Paul Green's slyest move," in the eyes of Drew Harris. "To make the relationship palatable by treating it on the comic level. How many people in those early audiences realized, do you think, when they felt a warm glow at the success of the relationship between Tom and Agona, that they were responding favorably to an interracial marriage? I'll bet not many."

For all that, from the perspective of 2000 the play in its early years retained vestiges of the stereotypical Indian associated with dime novels and B-movie westerns. When the Algonquians reassembled and met the English after the interruption of the harvest dance, they made themselves objects of audience laughter by the way they carried on over the trinkets distributed as gifts by the English (the Algonquian chief wore a cooking pot as a hat, and so on). When the chief was murdered by the English, the surviving medicine man expressed his grief through shrieks and wails and the flinging about of sand—actions that to the audience would seem strange, even outlandish, expressions of grief. In her single-minded pursuit of Old Tom, Agona was a parody of the lovesick female, and, as such, a frequent object of ridicule. And the Algonquians with speaking parts in the play spoke a pidgin English now called Tonto (in honor of a well-known practitioner, the Lone Ranger's faithful Indian companion), saying things like: "Wanchese have no brother. Wanchese brother Wingina—white men kill. Wanchese never forget. When moon come big white men be gone" (where Wanchese was the speaker, Wingina the chief killed by the English [1937, p. 69]).

With a rising acceptance of the humanity of Native Americans in the larger society, the stereotypical streak in *The Lost Colony* weakened the impact of the play on contemporary audiences. Realizing this, Drew Harris set out to do something about it. In his three years as artistic director, he eliminated the gift-giving, hence the clowning, when the Algonquians and English first meet. Audiences can now empathize with the grief of the medicine man as he cradles the head of the dead chief in his lap and moans, calling out Wingina's name in a voice of lamentation. Simply by casting her as a pretty young woman and eliminating her slapstick gestures, Harris transformed Agona from an object of ridicule to a strong positive character, whose presence adds believability to the spiritual growth of Old Tom (an important development in the play). He even created a tender moment between the two when, building on the artistic talent she always possessed (she makes candles for the colonists' chapel), Agona brings out a necklace she has made, places it over Tom's head, and gently arranges it on his shoulders.

For the only dialogue changes in the humanization of the Algonquian characters, Harris took a cue from history. Historically, the first Algonquians to learn English were two young men (Wanchese and Manteo) who returned to England with the first party of explorers in 1584 and remained there the better part of three years in the household of Raleigh before returning with the last group of settlers in 1587. These young men would have learned English not by listening to the radio or going to the movies in the 1930s but by talking with their sixteenth-century English companions during a voyage of several weeks to England, nearly three years in London, and a lengthy voyage back to Roanoke Island. Realizing this, Harris translated their speeches from the Tonto pidgin into the language spoken by the English characters in the play. Hence in the 2000 season Wanchese said: "I have no brother. Wingina was my brother and you white men killed him. This I shall never forget. Upon the full moon every white man will be gone" (2000 acting script, p. 30).

At intermission I mentioned changes such as these to the man next to me from Long Island, and he wondered if Paul Green ever altered the play like that. "Sure," I said, and told him the funny story about the death of Ananias Dare.

In the play, Dare is the military captain Eleanor White's father induces her to marry for reasons of social status despite her reciprocated love for a young tenant farmer, John Borden. Dare is killed in a battle with Indians, and subsequent events push Eleanor and John together. For audiences, a gratifying development at the end of the play is that finally, in the egalitarian society of Roanoke Island, the love of Eleanor and John is free to flourish.

In the years before World War II, however, Dare's death was not shown on stage. He was last seen leading a party of soldiers off stage in pursuit of attacking Indians. Then the Historian read out the names of the colonists killed in battle, Dare's name among them. And in those years Green occasionally got scolding letters from people disturbed—you could almost see a finger wagging—disturbed that he would show a married woman carrying on like that with another man when her husband must be somewhere about. Such behavior flew in the face of all morality, these correspondents felt, and made the play an encouragement of infidelity. What on earth was Green thinking about, they demanded—which means, of course, the letter writers had missed Dare's name in the list of those killed in battle.

Because of the war, *The Lost Colony* did not play in the summers of 1942, 1943, 1944, and 1945, and during that time Green made several changes in the play, a notable one in the staging of Dare's death. Beginning with the reopening in 1946, Dare still led his troops off in pursuit of the Indians, but then audiences saw him stagger back on stage, an arrow clearly visible in his back as he spun and fell and expired, his head in the lap of his wife, who in a few new lines announced to the colonists—and the audience, and the world at large—that her husband was dead. For over fifty years, through the 1999 season, this very public death was made even more so by where it was played—down front on center stage right in the lap of the audience. The 2000 production, in a nod to subtlety, moved the death back to the deep right side of the stage. "But the arrow's still there," said my neighbor from Long Island when the episode came around. And there was enough staggering and exclaiming so that no one could miss the event. My neighbor was chuckling during the episode, then whispered: "Sorry. I couldn't help thinking how it came about. Usually I don't laugh when somebody dies on stage."

Just as act 2 started, the little girl behind me, looking over her mother's shoulder toward the back row of seats, called out, "Look at that man waving his arms up there!" This embarrassed her mother, but the child, unengaged with the performance for a moment and looking exactly opposite to the presumed direction, had spotted part of the support system of the show, an element of the production most people at a play know little about. Any production involves more than meets the eye of the audience (in the work of directors, designers, managers, technicians, crews, and the like). But *The Lost Colony* is unusual in the elaborateness of its support requirements. Doing the play outdoors brings a range of challenges related to weather that the typical regional or Broadway theater never faces. And having a cast of performers numbering around a hundred means that in scale the operation dwarfs the usual professional show, where a large cast might number fifteen to twenty and the usual cast numbers in single digits. While caught up in a performance, audience members should not be wondering how all the pieces of the show came together. Afterward, however, while savoring the experience, they might legitimately wonder. And at *The Lost Colony* so much goes on over the heads and behind the backs of the audience that it makes a subject in its own right.

Start with the obvious: weather. At *The Lost Colony* rain has been a concern literally from day one. In his diary for July 4, 1937, Paul Green noted that "at last" the play had opened, but with the "agony of rain in first act." Any number of years later few people think of attending a performance without a question running through their mind about the likelihood of rain. How do the managers at *The Lost Colony* deal with this fact of life?

As her title suggests, Beth Stewart as production manager has overall responsibility for day-to-day operations. During the 2000 season I talked with her several times, and she explained to me that on the question of rain "danger, not dampness, is the issue." She is concerned for the welfare of the audience, cast, crew, scenery, and props. "We can play through light showers and nobody minds," she said. "Audiences for the most part are glad to sit it out, even reluctant to go back to the covered concession areas to wait out a shower. If it's raining more than a little bit at 8:30, we'll delay the opening a few minutes (though the whole company is in place and ready to start by 8:25 sharp, regardless of the weather). If a hard rain comes up during a performance, we suspend things a while. A hard rain makes it unsafe for the dancers and people in fight scenes, and the audience can't hear much either. So we suspend things for up to thirty minutes. But the real problem is lightning. An electrical storm anywhere about—we watch that pretty closely."

A few afternoons later I learned what she meant by "watch that pretty closely" when Tama Creef walked me through the sound and lighting setup of the show and, with the help of master electrician Matt Strampe, gave me what Matt called "Sound and Light Design 101." (Tama's title is education manager, but—though I did indeed get an education that afternoon—her title signifies other kinds of educational work, with schools, for instance, and civic groups interested in *The Lost Colony* and the history it commemorates.) During a performance, lights are managed from the control booth, a two-level rectangular building running parallel to the back rows of seats and several feet behind them. On the ground level of the control booth is the station where Beth and others watch electrical storms—and all other weather features too.

The station is a computer with Intellicast software that gives constant access to the Doppler radar we are all familiar with from the Weather Channel or the weather forecast on the nightly television news. At *The Lost Colony* the Doppler signal originates in Charlotte, North Carolina—less than a degree south of the latitude of Manteo and 329 miles west—and sweeps an arc that cuts across Chesapeake Bay in the north and the upper coast of South Carolina in the south. About 6:30 each evening the computer is turned on for a spot check of the weather. Experienced weather watchers can tell ground clutter from fog and haze, and storm systems with only rain from dangerous thunderheads (Doppler shows these different things in different colors). Spot checks continue through the evening unless there is something to watch, in which case the storm is monitored continuously for its size, nature, speed, and direction. "Out here on Roanoke Island most weather fronts come in from the west in the summer," Tama said. "While we get our share of storms—and if they're electrical, we cancel and get everybody out of here—it frequently happens that Albemarle Sound carries storms north of us. It can be raining on the beach at Nags Head and Kitty Hawk and on up toward Corolla, and we won't get a drop."

Beth Stewart and the production stage manager (in the 2000 season, David Rosenberg) make the call about delaying, suspending, or cancelling a performance. "We can't manage the weather," Beth said. "But we can manage the situation with pretty good awareness of what the weather will do. We'll know, for instance, whether we're in for two hours of rain or only a shower that'll be out of here in ten minutes. That tells us whether to cancel or just hold off a little while. And we know, if a bad storm gets out over Albemarle Sound and is still headed at us, we're in trouble. When that happens toward the end of a performance, David can speed things up and try to get us out of here before the storm hits." (Alerted by the production stage manager, the cast speeds up its delivery of lines and movement through the action, and David himself picks up the pace of cues. Rehearsals have been devoted to this quickened pace, just as football teams practice two-minute drills, so performances are smooth even if a little faster. In a play on an old theatrical label for final rehearsals, the cast calls these accelerated performances "run throughs.")

The rain policy of *The Lost Colony* is printed on the back of every ticket to every performance. "Performances are never cancelled before 9:00 P.M.," the statement begins. Then in bold type on a separate line: "No refunds." Followed by the pledge: "Exchanges will be granted by calling our Box Office at 1-800-488-5012." Tama, who managed the box office for several years, said that after a rain-out, between a quarter and a half of the ticket holders come back the next night for an exchange, "which can really put a squeeze on things." After that, the box office doesn't keep records on exchanges. Since the offer of exchange is good for the life of the ticket holder, not just the season in which the ticket was bought, additional exchanges dribble in during subsequent days, weeks, even years.

The economic impact of rain is easy to see if you visit Carolyn Spallino, accounting supervisor at *The Lost Colony*. The Waterside Theatre has been substantially rebuilt three times since 1937, each time with the incorporation of new design elements aimed at improving acoustics and sight lines for the audience. This has meant moving the center stage and the two side stages closer to the audience, increasing the angle of elevation of the seating floor, and eliminating seats—from 2,500 in 1937 to 1,600 at present. Using her records for the 2000 season, Carolyn Spallino showed me what rain meant. "Eleven hundred, twelve hundred tickets—anything from there to a sellout is a good night," she said. Pointing to the computer screen: "See, last Thursday, 1,182 tickets, for a box office of $15,420. Friday and Saturday nights are usually big. What if we'd had a rain-out Thursday night—we didn't, thank goodness—and half those people showed up the next night or two to claim their exchange? We could have been out as much as seven, eight thousand dollars for tickets we could have sold if they hadn't been exchanged."

"In recent decades you've had something like seventy scheduled performances a season," I said. "What's the record number of rain-outs?"

Beth Stewart was in the conversation and said: "Ten, in 1975. That year the cast nicknamed it *The Moist Colony*. Two or three rain-outs a season is the norm, but this year we're ahead of that already." (The 2000 season would experience eight rain-outs.)

If rain is a headache at *The Lost Colony*, financially and otherwise, hurricanes are everybody's worst nightmare. Fortunately, along the southeast coast the big month for hurricanes is September, after the play has closed (although hurricanes can do major damage in the off-season, as was the case in 1960 when a mid-September hurricane demolished the Waterside Theatre and initiated one of the major rebuilding phases). But every three or four years a hurricane makes landfall, or threatens to, in August. A threat anywhere from South Carolina to Virginia cuts down on the beach population, depriving *The Lost Colony* of income for weeks (people are slow about returning to the beach after a hurricane).

If the storm poses a realistic threat to Roanoke Island and evacuation is advisable, that adds a pretty penny to the cost of doing business. Cast and crew, typically about 125 people, are moved inland a safe distance, usually to the Greenville area 120 miles west, where they are put up in motels at company expense while continuing to receive contracted salaries. Such an evacuation last occurred in July 1996. The most recent bad brush with a hurricane was in 1998, when Hurricane Bonnie made its way slowly up the Carolina coast in late August. The last scheduled performance that season was Friday, August 28, but the last performance to get on was Monday, August 24. Tuesday at 6:34 A.M. mandatory evacuation of Roanoke Island was ordered. That day crews hurriedly dismantled and stored the set and equipment, then everyone was dismissed to go home. The last four performances of the season were cancelled.

Humidity, less of a drag on the bottom line than rain or hurricane, is a weather issue every night, since it strongly influences the quality of sound. At *The Lost Colony* sound (spoken dialogue and singing) is picked up by microphones placed in all areas of the stage and projected through a system controlled from a soundboard right behind the last row of seats. The soundboard is an elaborate version of what you have on your car radio, where with a knob or two you balance treble and base and alter the volume. On the soundboard are about two dozen equalizers (dials with numbered settings) for balancing high-, mid-, and low-range sounds from the area mikes and about a dozen faders (levers across the bottom of the board) for raising and lowering volume. To set the equalizers and faders and adjust them during a performance, a sound engineer must take into account humidity and temperature. If humidity is low, say 48 percent, with a temperature in the 70s, settings for equalizers and faders will differ considerably from what they would be if humidity were high, say 75 percent or higher, with a temperature in the 80s. Generally, the higher the humidity, the greater the demand on the projection system.

And on the cast as well. No matter how good the electronic projection system, voices weakly supported by singer or speaker sound weak. And as humidity increases, so does the difficulty of breathing deeply and maintaining breath support for the voice. Paul Laprade went into this with me one night following a performance. Music director and arranger at *The Lost Colony* in 1999 and 2000, Paul is a graduate of the Eastman School of Music and Westminster Choir College, and the twenty-member chorus for the play has tended over the years to consist largely of Westminster students. Each night during the performance, he stands near the soundboard just behind the last row of seats and conducts all of the singing in the play (hymns, folk songs, and other early English music are prominent features of the production) and also the choral speaking of the Historian's lines (so he was "that man waving his arms up there" spotted by the little girl looking the wrong way). When I asked about the need for his nightly effort, he explained that speakers or singers were sometimes too far apart to stay in sync by ear. Especially was this true for the choral speakers, who did not have a musical beat to follow and relied on his beat altogether for precisely coordinated enunciation. "And humidity just makes everything harder—breathing, projecting, hearing. Standing up here, I know what the audience hears. Let the humidity get up into the 70s or above and I slow the beat a little and start sweeping my arms down lower and lower to remind singers and speakers they must work harder at breathing deeply and projecting."

Weather even determines the kind of fireworks display the audience sees. It can be spectacular, with a quarter of a minute of booms, bangs, and whistling sizzles as rockets streak into the night sky and burst into plumes and pinwheels and globes of colored blazes that drift gently down before some of them explode again and broaden the beautiful shower. The display comes in the first act as the Queen entertains the common people of England (and the play entertains children in the audience and adults like me). But if you are sitting in the audience some night and feel a pretty good breeze in your face, you can forget about the A-1 version of the display.

On the back side of the stage is a pier extending maybe a hundred feet into Roanoke Sound, and fireworks take off from the end of the pier out over the water. Rockets are of two kinds. Titanium salutes, used at start and finish of the display, boom like thunder and explode into tight showers of white sparkles. Flights-of-three, not so loud, fill the sky with points of streaking colored fires—red, green, blue. Out at the end of the pier, rockets sit in mortars that are themselves wired to a switchboard on the back of the set, where each launch is triggered. The pyrotechnician (in the 2000 season, Michelle Johnson) works just behind the set, not a hundred feet out over the water, so she can see the red light on a wall above her that transmits cues from the production stage manager, who controls the timing of her launches. She sets up a full array of fireworks for each performance, but wind and moisture determine how much of it, and which kinds, she can use.

The usual wind at *The Lost Colony* is out of the west or southwest, but occasionally it swings around to the northeast. A northeast wind blows from the ocean across the Outer Banks and Roanoke Sound directly into the theater and surrounding woods and is the wind audience members feel in their face. When I visited the backstage area, Michelle Johnson had a strip of green cloth fixed to a pole out on the pier to be sure of wind direction. Any northeast wind makes her nervous for its potential of blowing burning debris back over the audience and woods as it falls. When a northeast wind begins to call attention to itself (at *The Lost Colony* they judge wind velocity by the seat of their pants, but probably a velocity of six to eight knots lets a wind call attention to itself), Michelle cuts out the flights-of-three, which have much the wider spread, and launches only titanium salutes. Let a northeast wind become a stiff breeze and she eliminates the salutes as well.

Moisture in the launching mortars (as might happen if a shower came along early in the play or humidity is high) is another problem, regardless of wind direction. Such moisture causes low breaks—rockets going up only a little way before exploding or shooting off crazily in some horizontal direction. "When that happens," Beth Stewart told me, "cast members have instructions to duck. Audiences do that instinctively." She said two low breaks occurred during the 2000 season, on nights of high humidity. Usually moisture in the mortars, like a stiff northeast wind, just causes Michelle to cancel the fireworks altogether.

In which case, she shoots off a shotgun.

I mentioned that the production stage manager could pick up the pace of a performance in the face of an oncoming storm. When I heard this, I was curious how he did it. During a performance, the PSM works out of the control booth, a two-level building several feet behind the last row of seats. On the first level are storage areas and the computer with the Doppler radar hookup. The top level, reached by ladderlike steps, is open across the front from roofline down to the top of a desk. The space is divided into two compartments, side to side. On the left side, if you are looking down toward the stage, the master electrician controls the lightboard and two electricians operate follow spots. On the right side is the PSM's desk. One night I sat in the booth with him and realized that, as far as controlling performance tempo is concerned, he is like the conductor of a symphony.

David Rosenberg, production stage manager for the 2000 season, has wide experience in the professional theater and was the person who called my attention to the way *The Lost Colony*, with a cast of about a hundred, dwarfs the usual Broadway or regional theater production. He made the point while telling me about the difficulties of organizing a production of that scale, starting with rehearsals. For the 2000 season artistic director Drew Harris met the cast three weeks before opening night and, with David and other associates such as music director Paul Laprade, had that relatively short time to get the show in shape (a job made doable by the fact that about a third of the cast carried over from previous years — a typical occurrence). The trickiest part of the job in those three weeks may be scheduling scenes for rehearsal in such a way that you don't have the same actor in three places at once — say, in rehearsal hall A for one scene, on stage for another, and in rehearsal hall B for something else, all at 9:00 A.M.

David's desk in the control booth is a terrible place to experience the play. You are above the focal point of the sound system speakers and hear echoes, and on a level with most of the lights so that you are as much aware of the beams as of the objects they illuminate. But it is the perfect place to look down over the audience to the stage and see everything that happens. There is even a grandeur to the view since at that elevation you can see the stage silhouetted against a wide expanse of the sound from somewhere above Manns Harbor on the mainland in the west to Nags Head Woods on the Outer Banks in the northeast. And the sky, as it darkens and fills with stars, is huge.

On the night I spent in the booth the radar showed a line of showers and thunderstorms to the west of Roanoke Island and headed our way, so people kept a close check on the computer screen from 6:30 on. David and I climbed up to his desk about 8:00, and he got things in order. He had a clipboard with a form dated for that night's performance on which he would note the minute each act started and finished and jot comments about strong and weak points in the show (for compliments or extra work). The clipboard also carried a three-column list, the columns headed "Character," "Actor," and "Understudy," with names running down two and a half pages under the headings. (Each major role has two or three understudies, and several actors understudy two or three parts.) He also had a script heavily marked up in different colors for the different kinds of cues he gives. And he had a headset that gave him two-way communication with the house manager, the soundboard operator, the lightboard operator, the left stage manager, and the right stage manager.

Just before putting on the headset, he smiled, I thought, apologetically: "You sure you want to sit through this? People think of the theater as glitz and glamour. I promise you, there's none of either in the work up here."

"Nuts and bolts," I said, "what goes on behind the scene, background— all the things people *don't* think about while they watch a performance, that's what I'm after." I shifted positions in the armless metal chair and got my notebook laid out on the desk.

About 8:20 David checked with the house manager and learned that the crowd was large that night and many people were still coming in. He asked her to have the ushers hurry the seating along. Then he spoke with the two stage managers (who operate behind the scene on either side of the stage) and was told that the actors were in place and ready for the opening. A minute or two before 8:30 he announced over the public address system that taking photographs during the performance was prohibited and that the part of Father Martin in that night's performance would be played by Eric Green (an understudy). Then he told the lightboard operator to take down the houselights. In the moment of darkness in the theater, actors filled the stage, and David put down 8:32 on the time sheet. Then he said "go." Simultaneously, stage lights and accompanying music came up, and, Paul Laprade conducting, the cast raised their voices in the opening hymn.

For the rest of the evening David was mostly watching the performance carefully and calling cues. He calls three kinds: for the stage managers, for the soundboard operator, and for the lightboard operator. All the cues follow the same format: "stand by for X," then "go." In his copy of the acting script, the spot for each "stand by" is marked in colored ink (a red, green, or black X in the text with an arrow to the full cue written in a margin). His sense of timing dictates the following "go," when the cue is acted on. For the stage managers he cues the entrance of actors and special effects such as battle noises, the majestic arrival and departure of the sailing ship, and the fireworks display. So as not to confuse things, he differentiates light and sound cues by using numbers for lights and letters of the alphabet for sound (thus in his script the first of each kind is written as "L Q—1" and "S Q—A.") Light cues are the most numerous, since the lights change frequently in color, direction, and intensity to support changes of mood and focus on stage, and David's script frequently has a notation such as "Stand by L Q—27–30," followed by "27—go, 28—go," and so on.

The foul weather skipped us that night. At 9:00 someone who had been watching the Doppler screen came up to tell David the line of storms was staying north of the sound, miles from us. In a few minutes we could see tiny bolts of lightning so far away there was no trace of thunder, while overhead our sky was full of stars. So I didn't get to see a "run through" (though from watching David pace the show with his cues, it was easy enough to understand how he sped things up when need be). With a southwest wind, however, the fireworks that night were tremendous. At intermission the right stage manager called to tell David a light needed in act two had been broken during a scene shift (it was a light fitted with colored gels to simulate fire under a cook pot, with an attached smoke cone), and he sent an electrician down to fix it. The left stage manager also called to say an actor was having an adverse reaction to a recent tattoo (nauseated, I believe she said) and wasn't sure he could go on for the second act. David checked his cast and understudy list, gave her a name, then withdrew it and asked her to alert a second person when he realized the first understudy had already stepped into another role. As it turned out, the original actor was not too sick and played his part through to the end. The end came as "Stand by L Q—140. (Pause.) 140—go." House lights came up and the theater filled with applause as David put down 10:51 on the time sheet.

At that point on July 20, I was part of the audience filling the theater with applause. My neighbor from Long Island was on his feet applauding too, and vigorously. "Wow!" he said. "You won't see anything like this on Broadway. Where else can you find a great show that puts you in mind of what we're about as a country? And look at the stars! We'll be back."

I wished him and his wife a good stay on the Outer Banks and a safe trip home and made my way out of the theater with the crowd. Outside, everyone stayed on the wide path to the parking area as I veered off to the right on a narrow path through the woods for maybe a quarter of a mile to the National Park Service buildings where I had left my car. This is one of my favorite walks. By no means a wilderness such as the colonists found (the Park Service maintains low lights along the paved walk and keeps grass growing), the grounds are filled with trees—taller pines with an understory of dogwoods, hollies, black gum, and live oaks draped with Spanish moss. You never encounter many people there and can concentrate on the smell of leaf mold and the wind soughing in the trees.

That night no one else was around, and I remembered Beth Stewart's story from her first summer at *The Lost Colony*, when she worked twenty-hour days as a stage manager and one night after the show fell asleep on the set. When she woke up around three in the morning, she couldn't get her bearings for a moment and was sure a crowd of colonists were there in the moonlight peering down at her in a puzzled way—colonists, or their ghosts. I felt the presence of spirits myself that night as I walked along, spirits of the daring English people who set in motion the making of a democratic society, of the perplexed but initially hospitable Algonquian people who met them right here under trees like these, and of the people centuries later who pioneered another new thing, a kind of theater, and still work to sustain it.

A NOTE ON THE TEXT

Since the early 1920s Paul Green had dreamed of writing a play about the Roanoke colonists, and in 1921, while a student at the University of North Carolina in Chapel Hill, he went to Roanoke Island to watch the making of a film about the colonists funded by the North Carolina legislature for use in state schools.[1] In the early 1930s interest in memorializing the colonists gained momentum among leaders in coastal North Carolina, and whether from Chapel Hill, where he lived, or New York City, where he went for productions of his plays, or Hollywood, where he went to write motion picture scripts, Green stayed in touch with the situation through correspondence with W. O. Saunders, editor of the Elizabeth City *Independent*, D. B. Fearing, state senator from Manteo, and others.[2] By late 1936 Saunders, Fearing, and other members of the Roanoke Island Historical Association had committed themselves to the production of what they called a pageant during the summer of 1937 in conjunction with the 350th anniversary of the Roanoke settlement in 1587. In January 1937 they visited Green in Chapel Hill and, thinking of their production as a one-year affair, drew up a simple contract with him to write the work.[3] Green wrote *The Lost Colony* during the early months of 1937 and in June took the script with him to Roanoke Island for rehearsals leading to the opening on July 4.

Over the next few decades Green published three editions of *The Lost Colony*, all issued by the University of North Carolina Press. The first edition, published in early August 1937, was ready for sale during the inaugural season. The second edition, published in June 1946, to coincide with the reopening of the play following World War II, incorporated changes to the script made during the seasons from 1937 to 1941 and also revisions Green made in preparation for the reopening (such as the staging of the death of Ananias Dare). The third edition, published in June 1954, continued the

1. For his account of the trip, see *A Southern Life: Letters of Paul Green, 1916–1981*, ed. Laurence G. Avery (Chapel Hill: University of North Carolina Press, 1994), 58–66.

2. For a letter to Saunders, see *A Southern Life*, 209.

3. For the contract, see *A Southern Life*, 269–70.

process of textual development by incorporating Green's revisions since 1946 (such as deletion of the brief encounter between Walter Raleigh and William Shakespeare in act 1, scene 4).

In addition to the three published editions of the play, there is a yearly run of production scripts, unpublished but maintained by the Roanoke Island Historical Association. In the prewar years, and following the war into the early 1950s, Green was much involved with annual productions of the play, sometimes operating almost like an artistic director himself. Consequently, during those years he was responsible for departures in production from the published text (and would incorporate most of them the next time the play was published). From the late 1950s onward, however, he became less directly involved in yearly productions, in part because by then he sometimes had seven or eight outdoor historical plays running each summer in various parts of the country and could not devote himself exclusively to any one of them. Nevertheless he stayed in touch with *The Lost Colony* and, according to the record in the 2000 production script, approved of revisions initiated by Joe Layton in 1967 and 1971, the last times the production script was revised before Green's death in 1981. (Among the revisions were the removal of the Historian from his cubicle and also a reversal of the order of scenes 4 and 5 in act 2 so that the scene in the queen's palace—scene 4 in published editions—became scene 5 in the production script.)[4]

Another text is important too. In 1980 Green went back to work on *The Lost Colony* and carefully reconsidered it. He based his work on the most recent published edition, that of 1954, but made numerous changes. For one thing, he checked names, dates, and other historical facts underpinning the play and corrected the few historical inaccuracies that had persisted in all texts. An example is the name of the pilot of the ship that transports the colonists from England to Roanoke Island. The pilot is a prominent character in the play, and from the first Green called him Simon Fernando. In 1980, however, he discovered that the last name was Fernandes and—though it has no performance value—for the sake of accuracy changed the spelling accordingly.[5] Other sorts of changes occurred in the dialogue. In the speeches

4. Something of the interplay between production scripts and published editions is represented in *History Into Drama: A Source Book on Symphonic Drama*, ed. William Free and Charles Lower (New York: Odyssey Press, 1963).

5. For the pilot's name and other information about the historical colonists, see William S. Powell, "Who Were the Roanoke Colonists?," in *Raleigh and Quinn: The*

of Old Tom, Green reinserted folk sayings and biblical allusions cut in the past to shorten running-time. (The sayings and allusions typically suggest a context for viewing a particular character or action.) In conversations between John Borden and Eleanor White/Dare he allowed fuller expression of their feelings for one another (though by today's standards that love affair may still seem restrained). He reinserted the brief encounter between Raleigh and Shakespeare in act 1, scene 4, and the episodes of individual suffering in the last scene of the play. And he maintained the order of scenes in act 2 as it is in all published editions of the play, not reversing the order of scenes 4 and 5 as the production script had done. But from the production script he took the handling of the Historian, who was no longer confined to his cubicle and delivered his lines from one place or another on the forestage.

Green did not publish the 1980 text but printed and bound a few hundred copies at his own expense as gifts for family members and friends. Of existing texts of the play (published or unpublished), the 1980 text is historically the most accurate and provides the fullest development of characters, action, and theme. It also represents the last stage in the evolution of the play in the mind of its author. As Green took the 1954 edition as the basis for the 1980 text, I have taken the 1980 text as the basis for the present edition.

The kinds of changes I have made in that text are outlined here. I have repaired what seem to me oversights or typographical errors in the language of the 1980 text. Also for the pidgin English (Tonto) still spoken by Manteo and Wanchese in the 1980 text I have substituted the normal English of the 2000 production script. And I have followed the production script by having the men, women, and children of the colony declare, in the climactic scene at the end of the play, "And we'll be free!" rather than "And we'll be men!" as in the 1980 text. Such changes grow out of my sense that *The Lost Colony* is an ongoing enterprise in the present day and has its real existence in its relationship with a living audience.

Two final matters stem from the fact that my edition offers a reading text of the play. First, I have not eliminated the Historian and distributed his lines among appropriate characters. On stage, choral speaking can be very effective, with different characters taking bits and pieces of lines, sometimes speaking alone, sometimes in groups, sometimes moving straight through a speech, sometimes repeating key words and phrases for emphasis. I found the choral speaking of the 2000 production among its fine, strong elements.

Explorer and His Boswell, ed. H. G. Jones (Chapel Hill: North Caroliniana Society, 1987), 51–67.

On the page, however, such a breaking up of lines is primarily a source of confusion for the reader, and I have retained the Historian and his lines as the 1980 text presents them.

The other matter relates to stage directions. In a reading text, stage directions are essential as an aid to the reader in visualizing what happens on stage. It is instructive, however, that production scripts have no stage directions. That is the case because in any given season the director may change some of what is done on stage depending on his or her intentions and personnel. Any set of stage directions thus represents only one among a range of possibilities for stage action and should be so understood. By and large I have retained stage directions from the 1980 text (in which, incidentally, *left* and *right* are used from the point of view of an actor on stage, not from the point of view of the audience). I have simplified the directions, however, by paring down overly detailed descriptions of Indian dances and other gatherings throughout the play, and eliminating nonessential details, such as that a character is plump when there is no call within the action for that to be the case. In a few instances I have also added brief stage directions when the dialogue implied an action that had been left undescribed.

The foregoing sketch of the history of the text of *The Lost Colony* should make clear that the play has evolved over the years in response to audience needs and growing realizations of its artistic potential. The sketch should also make clear how the current edition fits into the evolutionary process.

The Lost Colony

SCENES

ACT 1

Scene 1: Prologue

Scene 2: An Indian village on Roanoke Island, summer 1584

Scene 3: A tavern yard in London, some weeks later

Scene 4: England, Queen Elizabeth's garden, the same day

Scene 5: King Wingina's village on Roanoke Island, summer 1586

Scene 6: England, a wharf in Plymouth, spring 1587

ACT 2

Scene 1: The fort in the Citie of Raleigh on Roanoke Island, July 1587

Scene 2: The same, later in the summer, 1587

Scene 3: The same, the following Sunday

Scene 4: England, a room in the queen's palace, autumn 1587

Scene 5: The fort on Roanoke Island, autumn 1588

Scene 6: The same, Christmas, 1588

CHARACTERS
(In the order of their appearance)

The Historian

Wingina, *an Indian chief*

Uppowoc, *an Indian medicine man*

Manteo, *an Indian chief*

Wanchese, *an Indian chief*

Manteo's Wife

Manteo's Son

Captain Phillip Amadas

Captain Arthur Barlowe

A Priest

Old Tom, *a masterless man*

A Landlord

First Soldier

Second Soldier

Master of Ceremonies

Queen Elizabeth

Governor John White

Eleanor (White) Dare

Ananias Dare

Lord Essex

Sir Walter Raleigh

William Shakespeare

John Borden

Governor Ralph Lane

Simon Fernandes

George Howe

George Howe, Jr.

John Cage

Reverend Master Martin

Joyce Archard

Elizabeth Glane

Alice Chapman

Margery Harvie

Jane Jones

Margaret Lawrence

Dame Colman

Thomas Archard

Thomas Smart

William Wythers

Agona, *an Indian woman*

First Artisan

Second Artisan

Virginia Dare

A Messenger

A Sentinel

A Runner

Mark Bennett

also

Indian Youths

Indian Maidens

Indian Men and Women

Milkmaid Dancers

Heralds

Courtiers

Ladies-in-Waiting

Pages

Sailors

Soldiers

Women Colonists

Men Colonists

Children

ACT 1

(It is the evening hour, and the audience is gathering in the amphitheatre for the play. As the twilight deepens and the vast vague shadow of night rolls in across the scene westward from the sea, the theatre music strikes up in a salutation of praise to Nature and Nature's Almighty God. As it plays, the lights in the amphitheatre go down and out. The overture concludes in a soaring fortissimo.

After an instant of silence the light comes up at the right front, revealing a group of some twenty or thirty men and women standing there. They are dressed in Elizabethan costumes and serve as both chorus and members of the colony to be. They break into a vibrant upswelling harmony.)

CHORUS.
    O God that madest earth and sky
    And hedged the restless seas around,
    Who that vast firmament on high
    With golden banded stars hath bound—

    O thou whose mighty arm doth keep
    The trembling world, the failing sun,
    Whose shining presence fills the deep
    Where lightless time's dark measures run—

    O God our Father, Lord above,
    O bright immortal, holy one,
    Secure within thy boundless love
    We walk this way of death alone,—Amen.

(As the singing dies away, the light fades down on the chorus and comes up at the front of the center stage to disclose the historian of the occasion who

stands illuminated in a circle of light. He is a kindly, elderly man, dressed in
a scholar's dark robe. He addresses a prayer out over the audience and into
the night.)

HISTORIAN.

O Lord, our heavenly Father,
Almighty and everlasting God,
In whom men have their life,
Their motion and their certain hope,
We ask the witness of Thy grace
Upon this sacred spot,
This bit of humble earth
Which we have come to dedicate.
For here once walked the men of dreams,
The sons of hope and pain and wonder,
Upon their foreheads truth's bright diadem,
The light of the sun in their countenance,
And their lips singing a new song—
A song for ages yet unborn,
For us the children that came after them—
"O new and mighty world to be!"
They sang,
"O land majestic, free, unbounded!"

(He bows his head, and the light dims down on him somewhat.)

CHORUS *(Chanting from the shadows.)*
This was the vision, this the fadeless dream—
Tread softly, softly now these yellow stricken sands.
This was the grail, the living light that leapt—
Speak gently, gently on these muted tongueless shores.

HISTORIAN *(As the light brightens on him again.)*
Now down the trackless hollow years
That swallowed them but not their song
We send response—
"O lusty singer, dreamer, pioneer,
Lord of the wilderness, the unafraid,
Tamer of darkness, fire and flood,

Of the soaring spirit winged aloft
On the plumes of agony and death—
Hear us, O hear!
The dream still lives,
It lives, it lives,
And shall not die!"

(The music strikes up in a sudden bold announcement. The historian stands, with bowed head, the light dimming down on him again and brightening on the chorus.)

CHORUS *(Chanting.)*
> The earth is the Lord's and all that therein is,
> The compass of the world and they that dwell therein,
> For he hath founded it upon the seas,
> And prepared it upon the floods.
>
> Glory be to the Father and to the Son
> And to the Holy Ghost—
> As it was in the beginning,
> Is now and ever shall be,
> World without end—Amen.

(After an instant of pause the light fades down on the chorus and comes up on the historian again. He opens his book, glances at it, then closes it.)

HISTORIAN *(Addressing the audience.)* Friends, we are gathered here this evening to honor the spiritual birthplace of our nation and to memorialize those brave men and women who made it so. Over four hundred years ago England—ever in competition with the growing power of Spain—determined to start her own colonization in the new world. On this Roanoke Island and at this very site a beginning was finally made, and from this beginning there has grown in time a new nation and a new form of government in the world. Here these early pioneers of that new order lived, struggled and suffered. And in the symbol of their endurance and their sacrifice, let us renew our courage and our hope. For as we keep faith with them so shall we keep faith with ourselves and with future generations everywhere who demand of us that the ideals of liberty and justice shall continue on the earth.

CHORUS *(Exiting.)* Amen, amen.

HISTORIAN. In the time of Queen Elizabeth the First, Sir Walter Raleigh, statesman, soldier, poet and favorite at the court, took the lead in plans for a permanent English colony in the new world. In April, 1584, he sent Captains Philip Amadas and Arthur Barlowe, with their Portuguese pilot, Simon Fernandes and two ships, to discover a fitting place for a first settlement.

Such a place they found on and around Roanoke Island, which they reached in late July, after a voyage of three months, and described as the goodliest land under the cope of heaven. It was the time of the harvest when they arrived, and the friendly Indians were celebrating and giving thanks and solicitations to their god.

(The light fades on the historian and holds as he turns and looks toward center stage, where a staccato drumbeat begins. The light comes up full and strong there.)

SCENE 2

(An Indian camp on Roanoke Island. Set in front of a line of palisades at the back are a few Indian houses roofed with bark and skins. At center stage is a wooden idol around which the celebration takes place.

To the left two Indian men are on their knees, one with a gourd rattle, the other with the drum that sets the rhythm of the ceremony. Squatted in a semi-circle in the middle foreground are a number of Indian women waving small leafy branches as they sway rhythmically with the drumbeats. To the right stands King Wingina, the Indian chief. He is a grave, majestic person about sixty years old. Over his shoulders drapes a fringed deer skin decorated with beads and shells. Behind him are his wife and a few attendants, and behind them are some warriors with bows, shields and spears. The king smokes a long-caned pipe as he watches the ceremony.

Uppowoc, the medicine man, performs before the idol, sometimes in dance step, sometimes in pantomime of activities that produce food — planting and harvesting, hunting, fishing. The tempo accelerates to a point where Uppo-

*woc's activities reach a climax, then slows. Six or seven young women enter
from the right to join the dance. They are dressed in short kirtles and in their
raised hands carry little baskets filled with ears of corn. They are met by a like
number of young men entering from the left and carrying a bow in one hand,
a simple field tool in the other—sharp stick, wooden mattock, wooden spade.
Twice the groups move back and forth before the idol, then place their baskets
and bows and implements on the ground in front of it and, with increasing
speed, begin running in place and waving their high-held arms and hands.
As the speed increases, all the spectators except the men with rattle and drum
are pulled into the dance before the idol. Suddenly the medicine man springs
to his feet, and all others fall to their knees. The medicine man goes among
them, moving his feathered sceptre over their bent forms. The rattle and drum
stop. The medicine man picks up ears of corn and one by one lays them before
the idol as an offering. As each one is laid, a drum tap accompanies it.)*

HISTORIAN *(Speaking from the shadows.)* Uppowoc, the medicine man,
   is asking his god what of the months ahead. Will the crops be plentiful?
   Will fish be bountiful for our hungry mouths? He calls on the great god
   of the sky to look upon them with favor.

*(Uppowoc piles more corn before the idol, toward which the kneeling people
reach supplicating hands. Then Uppowoc shows that the god has heard them
and promises good fortune.)*

HISTORIAN. The god is pleased with the gifts and worship of his people.
   Uppowoc lets them know there will be mighty crops of corn, two stalks
   to the hill. And fish! The nets will be loaded with them. So the god
   promises the people.

*(All the people begin to dance their thanks. Rattle and drum add their joy as
Uppowoc whirls among them all. Then off in the distance at the left the long
brazen note of an English horn is heard. The scene is convulsed to stillness.)*

HISTORIAN. But their god deceived them. Instead of plenteous crops
   and bounteous fish for the year ahead, these trusting people receive
   the Englishman.

*(The distant horn sounds again, and the theatre music begins a stately
English march. A gun is fired at the left, and the Indians flee toward the*

right, King Wingina and a few of his warriors in some dignity moving last. But at this moment an Indian runner enters from the left. He gives a loud "hooah!" and Wingina turns queryingly back. The runner dashes up to him, kneels, puts sand on his head and then springs to his feet. The other Indians in curiosity turn back also. The runner now pantomimes his message. The historian interprets.)

HISTORIAN. The runner tells of strange men yonder who have come in
  boats winged like birds.

(The runner flaps a piece of bright cloth in the air and indicates it was given him by the strangers who are coming there. He points off. Several girls rush up to look at the cloth. He gives it to his favorite. The march music now swells in volume. Wingina moves to center stage with great dignity and stands waiting, looking off to the left. The rhythmic tapping of a snare drum is heard there. The music swells, and Amadas and Barlowe, proud captains for the queen and Sir Walter Raleigh, enter. The historian stands at the far left front now in deep shadow as he looks on at the action. Soldiers in armor follow the captains. One bears a tall white cross, another an English flag. Following these are six other soldiers armed with halberds. The cortege stops at a signal from Amadas, and he walks forward to meet the Indian king. Amadas stops, extends his hand, then shakes hands with himself to illustrate, and once more extends his hand. Wingina smiles and nods, strikes his own head and breast with the flat of his hand and does the same to Amadas. Then the two shake hands. Amadas winces from the chief's grasp. Wingina takes a puff on his pipe and hands it to Amadas, who takes two or three puffs and hands it back. Clasping hands once more, the two kneel. Barlowe takes the cross and lowers it in blessing and consecration over the two leaders. The drum taps stop. Uppowoc, fearful of what is happening, hurries forward and shakes his sceptre menacingly at the cross. Wingina with a gesture orders him back, and he morosely retires. Amadas and Wingina now rise and embrace each other. The English march music has continued the while, and the historian watches the proceedings with keen interest from where he stands at the far left front. The chief now bends down and with a sharpened stone quickly cuts out a piece of turf. The runner hands him an arrow and he sticks it into the little square of turf and presents it to Amadas. The soldier steps forward with the English flag and holds it high aloft. The one with the cross does likewise. The medicine man makes one more effort with his sceptre to oppose the white and evil magic, but again Wingina gestures him back. Amadas hands the piece

of turf to Barlowe, then pulls a scroll from his belt, holds it up and reads in sonorous rolling words. The soldiers all stand at precise attention.)

AMADAS *(As the music softens.)* "In the name of our most sovereign Queen Elizabeth, by the grace of God, of England, France and Ireland, queen and defender of the faith: Know ye that of her special grace, certain science and mere motion, we do this day . . ."

HISTORIAN *(The speech passes to the historian. The light fades from center stage and brightens on him as he reads from his book.)* "We do this day take possession of this Island of Roanoke and the lands to the west, south and northward thereof to have and to hold for her and her assigns and successors and for her beloved and trusty servant, Sir Walter Raleigh, under her—forever! In the name of Almighty God— Amen!"

(The music sounds a flourish of trumpets, and the snare drum rolls as the historian moves farther downstage and turns again toward the audience. The music and sound end.)

HISTORIAN. And now with the flag planted proudly over a vast domain of wilderness, the explorers made ready to return to England, and many a young Indian brave wished to travel with them in their strange ships across the wide ocean to a land of great cities where the mighty queen sat on a throne shining like the sun. Lots were drawn and Wanchese, a kinsman of King Wingina, and Manteo, a young chieftain, were chosen. *(Music comments, then dies again. As the troops leave, Wanchese gives a farewell embrace to Wingina, as does Manteo to his wife and child, then the two young men hurry after the troops.)*

Back in England the explorers were received with great joy. Bells were rung, celebrations were held and ballads written about the new land. During their three-year visit, the two Indians, Manteo and Wanchese, were a marvel wherever they went, and tobacco smoking, which Sir Walter Raleigh introduced into the world, set the people agog. And even beggars on the streets, like our friend Old Tom himself, talked about the wonders beyond the seas.

(Light fades on the historian and comes up at the far left front.)

SCENE 3

(An open space in front of a tavern which is seen dimly in the background. A hullabaloo sets up in the tavern, and in a moment a beggarman, Old Tom, runs out, pursued by the landlord, a big burly man wearing an apron and carrying a stout cudgel.)

OLD TOM. Yeowee!

LANDLORD *(Swishing his cudgel through the air.)* So, it's more ale you want, eh? Get out, you thieving scoundrel! Get out of my tavern! Get out!

OLD TOM. Please, your reverence, I was sleeping all quiet there like a babe in the corner, 'mongst the kegs.

LANDLORD. Eigh, and sucking ale all night from the spigot drip. Where's your money?

OLD TOM. Please you, sir, I am but one of the Lord's poor anointed souls.

LANDLORD. One of the devil's gluttons, ye are. Stay out of my tavern.

(He shakes his cudgel threateningly, then turns back toward the tavern. Old Tom spits a bit of ale at the landlord, who feeling a drop of wetness on his neck glances up to see if it is raining. Then realizing the source, he turns with lifted cudgel, and Old Tom darts farther away. Disgusted, the landlord goes back into the tavern, and the lights come up fully on Old Tom. He is a poor specimen of masterless man, with rotting shoes, ragged breeches and tattered doublet. His hair under his battered hat is ill-kempt, and his thin face is marked with the ravages of exposure, penury and drink. He carries an ale cup in his hand.)

OLD TOM *(Forlornly and talking into the air.)* Lord-a-mercy, what's England coming to when a poor man can no longer beg a drink! "Get out, get out," the landlord says, "I have guests, visitors, lodgers—"

(He wanders toward center stage, the light staying with him.)

"all true followers of the queen and Sir Walter—coming to view the new wonders and make merry with her gracious majesty the queen." *(He pulls off his ragged hat and bows, speaking mockingly.)* Your gracious majesty! *(He lifts his ale cup to his lips but it is empty.)*

Hic—did I hear somebody say that all London is agog over the new world and Sir Walter Raleigh? It is in very truth—hah, hah! Then I am no longer lonesome, for they're all fools like me! And sure we must be merry, for in company there is merriment. *(He cuts a few spindle-legged capers and stops.)* Yet they are greater fools than I. For, item—do they not all run around with pipes in their mouths now and smoke pouring from the two chimneys of their noses, like their very liver were a roaring red-hot fire inside their bellies? Item—do they not go in great crowds, following after the two Indian kings like the twin sons of Noah had come back to rule the earth. And they're nothing but poor bedlam men—like myself, mayhap—out of the darkness of Africay. I know that. *(He breaks into a creaky laugh.)*

Then I should be knighted for me wisdom and set to walk in silver armor like the great Sir Walter. *(He draws himself up and marches comically back and forth, then stops and calls into the air.)*

Queen Elizabeth! Queen Elizabeth! Ah, she's busy thinking of the Spaniards. *(He calls again.)* Sir Walter Raleigh! Sir Walter Raleigh! Lord of Uppowoc and the new potato! Ah, he too is busy, dreaming of the new world. Well, look to your crowing, Sir Walter, *(He crows.)* or they'll cut your comb someday like his Worship, the Bishop! *(He shudders, then continues more quietly, as he gazes bleakly up at the sky.)* So, after all, I am a fool, for a fool is he who speaketh to shadows and getteth no answer. Then I tell it to God behind the shadows—between him and me is a great confidence—and God knows I be cold and hungry. *(He prepares to lie down on the ground.)* And now I lie down in his mercy and sleep on the poor man's bed whereon and wherein, blessed be his name, we shall all sleep together at the last day, and then there is neither fool nor wise man.

(He lies down, then sits up, for the music has begun playing the opening bars of his song. He sings.)

Hast thou heard what wise men say—
Every dog will have his day.
Come then, dogs, let's quick away—
(*There is a gap in the music while he looks about him and whistles for the dogs.*)
Hunting for our own.

Starved and homeless here we die.
Naked is the bed we lie,
Wisdom giveth us who cry
Nothing but a bone.

(*Sourly.*) Where is the bone?

(*While Old Tom sings, two soldiers with halberds and in full armor enter from the direction of the darkened center stage. They stop in surprise when they see the beggar.*)

FIRST SOLDIER (*Staring down at Old Tom and lowering his halberd.*)
Whist! Ye fool!

SECOND SOLDIER (*Sternly.*) Or we'll give thee a stone.

OLD TOM (*With gentle and vast irony—not surprised at all—pushes away the pointed head of the lowered and inimical halberd.*) Prithee, kind sirs, that rhymeth too close with bone—moan, groan—hic! hah, hah, hah! (*He raises his song again.*)

Wisdom's voice speaketh still—
Every Jack must have his Jill,
Man that's born of woman's ill
Hath no better wit.

But there cometh recompense—
(*The music pauses, he feels his pockets for the pence, holds out his hand to the soldier, who gives him a disgusted gesture, and the song resumes.*)
Unto fools who have no sense.
Death doth early take them hence—
That's the best of it!

(He stretches out on the ground again and is silent.)

FIRST SOLDIER *(Touching his nose as he steps back.)* Verily he smells like a
   fishmonger or a dealer in old cats. *(He pounds the ground with the staff
   of his halberd to rouse Old Tom.)* Heigh there!

SECOND SOLDIER. He sleeps like a dead clock. Let him rest.

FIRST SOLDIER. True, we'll wind him later.

SECOND SOLDIER *(Deprecatingly.)* 'Tis well known the great Sir Walter
   hath a soft heart for such.

OLD TOM. Aye, I hope so. He was once poor himself and may be so again.
   Likewise the queen. *(Murmuring.)* Poor queen.

FIRST SOLDIER. And why poor queen? For to be a queen is the height of
   heaven's favor.

SECOND SOLDIER. Aye, the very nadir and daystar of it.

OLD TOM *(Rousing himself again.)* Because as the world knows, the
   queen's power depends on the common people, and the common
   people are all poor. Aye, poor queen. *(Sighing.)* And Sir Walter too.
   Never will he make colony on Roanoke except through us. It is now
   the time of the demos—demos, that's the Greek for it—democracy,
   the rule of the people. It's writ in the sign of great waters.

FIRST SOLDIER. What waters, old fool?

OLD TOM. Cats that swim in the ocean will all drown. *(He lies down again.)*

FIRST SOLDIER. Well said and well hushed, old Abram man.

*(The two soldiers turn back the way they came as a flourish sounds in the
music. The light dies on Old Tom and comes up full on center stage.)*

SCENE 4

(Queen Elizabeth's garden, a gorgeous scene of flower beds and proper statuary of English heroes set here and there. Against an ivy-covered wall at the rear the queen's outdoor chair-throne is placed, and on either side of it two heralds in showy costumes are standing with trumpets in their hands. They lift the trumpets, and another flourish sounds, long and sustained. The theatre music strikes up a popular English melody of the times. The two soldiers now stand at attention on either side of the heralds. A number of court attendants enter from the right rear and stand lined up there. They carry pennons, gonfalons and a few coats-of-arms and in their brilliant uniforms are an impressive sight. They stand in motionless dignity through-out the scene. Jostling people now begin coming down the two audience aisles toward the center stage. These are the common folk of England—small shop-keepers, farmers, laborers, milkmaids, tapsters, tanners, sailors, masons, carpenters, joiners, thatchers, cobblers, smiths and a vagabond or two. Each group is led by a young man simulating a shepherd with a crook, and they all are singing as they come, aided by the theatre music.)

PEOPLE *(Singing.)*
We come from field and town,
From byre and forest green
In honor of the crown—
Honor of the crown
That fits our gracious queen.

From smiling field and down
We fragrant garlands glean
To weave a votive crown—
Weave a votive crown
That fits our gracious queen.

For England's great renown
Her virtue shines serene.
And love shall be the crown—
Love shall be the crown
That fits our gracious queen.

(The people move wonderingly and happily into the garden as their song ends. The master of ceremonies comes out from the right rear and takes his stand before the throne chair. His is the gaudiest clothing of all, with bright ribbons, high-heeled shoes and a tall hat, and in his hand he carries a long wand. He gives an exaggerated bow to the people and to the audience.)

MASTER OF CEREMONIES. Ladies and gentlemen, let it be known that I am the master of the queen's ceremonies, and in her majesty's name I bid you heartily welcome to this her garden party and special audience for you all. The evening is for merriment, and the queen mayhap will trip a lightsome toe herself.

(The crowd murmurs its joyous anticipation.)

You will shortly be initiated to wonders too, and then more wonders still, for down by the pond's edge is spread for all delight a most mar-velous repast—*(More murmurs of delight from the people)*—dishes of capons, sparrows and singing larks, roast boar's head and blackbirds and an oxen or two, topped off with barrels of sack, and also a new dish—*(Pausing for effect, then speaking satirically.)*—known as potato pie—a commodity lately brought from the new world and now the sudden taste of fashion and good form. Sir Walter Raleigh gives the feast.

(The people applaud and he shouts out.)

The queen approaches! *(Waving his wand.)* Let us hear music!

(A great flourish is heard again from the trumpets, and the crowd moves aside in expectancy. In the distance cannons are fired and then farther away still other cannons. The queen enters through a gate in the rear wall, preceded by two little flower girls scattering blossoms in her path. She is in a gorgeous costume similar to that shown in the National Portrait Gallery. The crowd kneels. Elizabeth is followed by two pages, three ladies-in-waiting and several courtiers. Governor John White and his daughter Eleanor and her fiancé, Ananias Dare, enter from the left, somewhat unnoticed. The queen seats herself on the chair-throne, under the officious supervision of the master of ceremonies. Suddenly she rises and spreads her arms out wide.)

QUEEN ELIZABETH *(In a loud clear voice.)* Unto my people, greetings!

A MAN'S VOICE. God bless our queen!

A WOMAN'S VOICE. Heaven keep her majesty!

OTHER VOICES. Give her long life, and a happy one!
England's glory forever she is!
Long live our queen!

(At a gesture from the queen the people rise.)

MASTER OF CEREMONIES *(In announcement.)* Your majesty—the most
excellent artist and cartographer, Master John White, gentleman, late
returned from that new land beyond the sea!

*(John White, a sturdy man of middle age, approaches the throne with his
daughter Eleanor, an attractive young woman of about twenty, by his side.
Ananias Dare, an aristocratic young man in his late twenties, accompanies
them. White carries a portfolio. The master of ceremonies continues.)*

His daughter, Mistress Eleanor White. Also your majesty's most loyal
servant, Captain Ananias Dare.

WHITE. *(The three bow before the queen, then White extends his portfolio.)*
To our queen and princess, these poor drawings of mine of Roanoke
Island in the new world. I pray they may bespeak my hope to serve thee
and Sir Walter Raleigh in the new world.

*(The master of ceremonies hands the drawings on to the queen. She looks at
them and passes them aside to a courtier.)*

ELIZABETH. Your talents are known to me, Master White. I may yet
command thy service.

(The people applaud.)

WHITE. Your majesty.

On the site where the Waterside Theatre was later built, 1936 (left to right): Paul Green of Chapel Hill, Melvin Daniels of Manteo, W. O. Saunders of Elizabeth City, Frederick Koch of Chapel Hill, and Chauncey Meekins, Martin Kellogg, Jr., D. B. Fearing, and Ike Davis, all of Manteo. (Paul Green Papers, Southern Historical Collection, University of North Carolina Library at Chapel Hill)

Ben Dixon MacNeill, publicist for The Lost Colony (left), and Paul Green inspect the unfinished stage of the Waterside Theatre, 1937. The plank foundation is visible beneath the sand. (Photograph by Ben Dixon MacNeill; North Carolina Collection, University of North Carolina Library at Chapel Hill)

The Waterside Theatre in its first season, 1937, with a dirt floor under backless wooden benches, the Historian's cubicle to the audience's left, and the choir stall to the right. (Photograph by Bayard Wootten; North Carolina Collection, University of North Carolina Library at Chapel Hill)

At the Manteo high school Paul Green discusses The Lost Colony *with Katherine Cale, who played Eleanor Dare, and other actors, 1937. (North Carolina Division of Archives and History, Raleigh)*

Women in hats, men in coats and ties, and children dressed as if for church watch Reverend Martin baptize the infant Virginia Dare (act 2, scene 3), 1937. Green described how the photograph was taken: "Representatives from The New York Daily News *came down to photograph the show. They ringed the sides and rear of the theatre with a little trough into which flash powder was poured and hooked it up with the camera in such a way that when the shutter was tripped, a great flare of light was provided." (Institute of Outdoor Drama, University of North Carolina at Chapel Hill)*

President Franklin Roosevelt (left) arrives at The Lost Colony *with Governor Clyde Hoey (center) and Lindsay Warren, U.S. congressman from Manteo's district, for the performance on Virginia Dare Night, 18 August 1937. (North Carolina Collection, University of North Carolina Library at Chapel Hill)*

Paul Green (left) and D. B. Fearing (center) with Eleanor Roosevelt following the opening night performance, 1939. (Institute of Outdoor Drama, University of North Carolina at Chapel Hill)

(He bows happily again and steps back. The queen looks out at Dare. She gestures toward him.)

ELIZABETH. Ah, Master Dare!

DARE *(Fervently.)* My queen! *(He falls to his knees, then rises and stands near White.)*

ELIZABETH *(To Eleanor.)* And thee, my child?

WHITE. Your majesty, my daughter. *(He leads Eleanor forward.)*

DARE *(Again fervently.)* My betrothed, your majesty, marking the union of two of thy most loyal houses. *(The queen extends her hand to Dare to be kissed. Eleanor kneels.)* Craving your blessing on the union, your majesty.

ELIZABETH. For your father's sake, Master Dare, and for your own, my blessing. *(Dare once more bows his fervent thanks.)* Ha, your father was a great soldier. *(Chuckling in reminiscence.)* La, how he could play at "The Shaking of the Sheets." *(Quickly.)* But that was before my time. *(She turns again to Eleanor.)* Fie, rise, my child. Beauty has its own claim to power.

(Eleanor rises and stands before the queen.)

WHITE. Pardon a father's pride, my lady, but excepting Sir Walter himself, none yearn toward the new land more than my maid.

ELIZABETH. A most foolish yearning for a maid, Master White. *(Eleanor, surprised, starts to speak, but the queen shifts the conversation abruptly.)* What say you, Master Dare? Is she not beautiful?

DARE *(With another sweeping bow, speaks unctuously.)* But lacking in that divinity that makes thee queen.

ELIZABETH. Master Dare is a good judge, but, I wager, a poor lover. *(Dare, a little puzzled, bows again as the crowd laughs politely.)* So,

Mistress Eleanor White, you are inclined toward Roanoke Island and the wilderness?

ELEANOR *(Curtseying.)* Yes, your majesty.

ELIZABETH. Why?

ELEANOR *(In a fresh strong voice.)* If England's men have dreams, so have her women.

ELIZABETH. Ho, what then, Master Dare?

DARE. If her men are England's power and glory, your majesty, then her women are her glory and power, and both in thee excelling.

VOICES. Long live the queen!

ELIZABETH *(With awkward pleasure.)* Flatterer. *(She tosses Dare a flower, which he catches gratefully, then turns again to Eleanor.)* And now, my child, no more of these mad thoughts. Leave the taming of the wilderness to sterner hands. Farewell.

ELEANOR. But your majesty . . .

ELIZABETH. *(Dismissing her with a gesture.)* Enough!

MASTER OF CEREMONIES *(Loudly.)* His most worshipful presence, Sir Walter Raleigh!

(A mumble of expectation and curiosity rises among the people, and they move forward only to be pushed back by the two soldiers. The trumpeters spontaneously sound a flourish. A second is begun. Elizabeth rises in vexation at this attention to Raleigh. She sits again as Sir Walter Raleigh enters from the left, dressed in gleaming armor. He is a tall, handsome man in his early thirties and is accompanied by the two Indians, Manteo and Wanchese. The former carries the square of turf, the latter a bundle of tobacco leaves and a large potato and is puffing his pipe. They both have dressed themselves up in a display of wampum and body markings for the occasion. Loud applause and exclamations of astonishment and wonder break out among the specta-

tors. *But the soldiers hush them down. Raleigh comes forward, bows and stands uncovered.)*

ELIZABETH *(With a wry smile.)* You seem to please the people well, Sir Walter, you and yours.

RALEIGH. I owe the people many thanks, your majesty.

ELIZABETH. Tut, tut, no doubt. But even so you're wise—there's safety in it.

RALEIGH. But safety most in the light of thy bright countenance, my queen.

ELIZABETH *(Smiling.)* You please me too, you strange and proud and dreaming man.

RALEIGH. I would you found nothing strange in my dreams, your majesty.

ELIZABETH. But I do. Know ye, we have an ancient foe that keeps us on our guard. All strength, all resources, all intent must be against Spain, and yet my nonpareil of valor, my fretful child, walks in his sleep, talks in his dreams of one thing only—the new world beyond the sea. But I am queen, and Philip is my enemy and being so I'll keep my soldiers, leaders, here—to break his power down and not to waste our purpose on some fancied empty wilderness. This for all the world to hear.

(The courtiers and people applaud vigorously.)

RALEIGH. I have a dream—so let it be, but still it will persist until I die. *(Gesturing.)* There in the sun that riseth strangely in the west I see the expiring phoenix of Spain.

ELIZABETH. I am no poet, Sir Walter. Speak plain.

RALEIGH. There is an ancient saying that if a tree would grow great it must send its roots deep and wide. In its shade the lesser trees will die. So it is with nations, so with an idea, or by your leave, a dream.

ELIZABETH. But first the tree must be made to live at its central heart. Such a tree is England. Or as a house, make its first foundation strong. Then build atop of it. But no more of these privy-public matters. Come.

RALEIGH *(In acquiescence.)* Your majesty.

ELIZABETH. Proceed.

RALEIGH *(Coming to Manteo and taking the turf.)* To thee, most gracious queen, I present this bit of earth in token of the new land which I have won in thy name. *(He hands it to her.)*

ELIZABETH. My brave knight beyond compare, you shall be rewarded.

(The people applaud more loudly than ever now, but the courtiers not so enthusiastically. She passes the turf on to a courtier.)

RALEIGH *(Bringing Manteo and Wanchese forward.)* These kingly subjects—Chief Manteo and Chief Wanchese—I now present to you, most gracious sovereign.

(The two chiefs incline their heads in recognition of the queen. The people crowd forward gapingly.)

Thy rightful sway and the sacred crown of England they do acknowledge. And out of the richness of the wilderness we offer these— *(He takes the tobacco leaves from Manteo.)*—the tobacco plant, sacred to the Indians—

(He hands the tobacco to Elizabeth, who smells it, makes a wry face, and hands it to one of the courtiers.)

—and this, an humble root—the potato.

(At the word "potato" a few titters are heard. It is handed up. Elizabeth takes it, looks at it, and passes it on to another courtier.)

ELIZABETH. But what of the vast mines of gold and silver and precious stones we reckoned on?

RALEIGH. These two may prove a greater source of wealth to your kingdom, your majesty.

ELIZABETH. La, Sir Walter, worse and worse. *(She looks at the long-stemmed pipe that Wanchese is smoking.)* So this is that wondrous smoking instrument. *(She reaches out, and it is handed up to her.)* Hum, it smells foul enough.

RALEIGH. Try it, your majesty. It is good for the vapors.

ELIZABETH *(Curtly.)* I have no vapors. *(She puffs at the pipe, then coughs.)* It bites like an adder. Hyeu!

(She falls to coughing and sputtering. Several of the ladies and courtiers surround her solicitously. Finally she recovers herself, throws the pipe back at Wanchese and looks angrily at Raleigh. But quickly recovering her dignity, she rises. The people fall to their knees.)

Conscious of the great worth of our loyal servant, Sir Walter Raleigh, and of all those brave and daring subjects who crossed the unknown sea to spread the name and conquest of England further, I accept this day the tokens of their loyalty and service. And I do designate and order that from this time forth the new and western empire shall be named— *(She pauses for effect while everyone listens in suspense.)*—"Virginia" in honor of myself, England's virgin queen.

(There is loud applause on all sides, and the trumpets break forth in a great flourish once more.)

VOICES. Long live the queen! Long live the queen! Long live the queen!

(Raleigh stands with bowed head looking at the ground. Elizabeth moves away at the left, the people rise, and the procession on the stage begins to go out after her.)

MASTER OF CEREMONIES. In honor of— *(Loudly.)* —the new land Virginia there will be fireworks, dances and games. And remember the feast to which you are invited. But only to the pond, no further, my good people. I counsel ye, be temperate, circumspect and of good bearing. And all will be well.

(He is barely able to get his speech out and is incontinently jostled by the hurrying crowd. In great dignity the two armored soldiers march out at the end of the procession. Attendants carry away the chair-throne at the rear. Sir Walter remains alone in the scene. The light stays on him. He paces back and forth a moment and then stands gazing disconsolately and a bit ruefully after the queen. A young man enters at the right front. He stops hesitatingly, then moves forward with an air of forced determination. He will address the great Sir Walter Raleigh, he will. But at this instant a group of laughing girls, dressed as milkmaids, enter at the left and gather dancing around Sir Walter, honoring him. The music is now a bright English folk dance, and the maids circle Sir Walter in rhythmic curtsies and skipping steps. He is much touched and blows a few kisses at them and now and then touches a lovely head as it turns by him. The dance ended, the maids run away as they came. Raleigh resumes his pacing. The young man hesitates once more and then comes forward. In the light he shows to be about twenty-one or -two, is somewhat shabbily dressed and, so far as appearances go, resembles any ordinary English youth of poor means in search of his fortune. He stops and bows.)

YOUNG MAN. Sir Walter Raleigh.

RALEIGH *(Stops his pacing and looks at him.)* What is it?

YOUNG MAN *(Handing him a note.)* Master James Burbage commends me to you.

RALEIGH *(Reading the note.)* So you hold horses at the theatre and make poetry? An odd combination—er—Master William Shakespeare.

YOUNG MAN. Aye, sir. It is an odd time and one must live. *(Grinning.)* By the horses, I mean, not poetry.

RALEIGH. So—and you are witty. Your home?

YOUNG MAN. From Stratford. I've lately come to London.

RALEIGH. And you would sail to Virginia?

YOUNG MAN. Yes, your honor.

RALEIGH. I fear you'd find no time for poetry there.

YOUNG MAN. 'Tis well. No one likes my poor verses here. Give me an ax, I can cut trees.

RALEIGH. You're wrong. Sir Philip Sidney has spoken to me of your talents.

YOUNG MAN *(Awed.)* The great Sidney!

RALEIGH. At the Mermaid Tavern he heard you and your ale mug reciting ballads. You have the gift of words, he said. Then cherish that gift. I will commend you to a friend, Master Shakespeare—one with money. *(Strongly.)* More than that, I will write a letter in your behalf at once.

YOUNG MAN *(Grabbing his hand enthusiastically.)* Then I am your debtor forever.

RALEIGH *(Gazing at him searchingly.)* You shall hear from me shortly. Farewell.

(The young man bows and goes away as he came. Raleigh stands for a moment, his head bent in thought. Then he turns and walks swiftly off at the rear. The light dims on the center stage and rises on the historian at the right front.)

HISTORIAN. So Shakespeare did not go to Roanoke Island, but that his imagination traveled to the new land is shown in some of his plays of later years. Thus it was that the young adventurous spirits of England were fired to Raleigh's dream.

(The light fades from the historian and rises on center stage at the left. A moment passes. The music reprises a bit of the milkmaid dance melody and dies. Eleanor White runs in at the left looking for Sir Walter.)

ELEANOR *(Calling.)* Sir Walter! Sir Walter!

(She looks around, picks up a flower and starts back the way she came. John Borden enters at the right. He is a tall, lithe young fellow about twenty-five or -six years old and of frank open face, tanned brown by the wind and sun. He

stops when he sees Eleanor. She seems to feel him there and after an instant turns and stares at him.)

John Borden!

BORDEN *(Doffing his cap in a crude bow.)* Your servant, ma'am.

ELEANOR. What brings you here?

BORDEN. Some matters of business only.

ELEANOR *(Brightly.)* And the farm—all goes well there?

BORDEN. It does. The harvest is thick on. The servants ask for you and the master—when will you return?

ELEANOR. At the queen's leave.

BORDEN *(With obvious moodiness.)* When you have had your fill— *(Waving his hand.)* —of this.

ELEANOR. Still those dark and bitter words, John Borden.

BORDEN. My tongue was ever wayward like my heart. You have cause to know that.

ELEANOR *(Now a little smilingly.)* Yes, wayward.

BORDEN. And most wrong, a certain captain of the queen's arms would say.

ELEANOR. John Borden!

BORDEN. But nay to that. *(Almost recklessly—after a pause.)* The wrong is hers who flies against the feelings of her heart.

ELEANOR *(Angrily.)* You dare accuse me.

BORDEN. Aye, my tongue at least is honest. *(He turns away.)* It speaks the truth— *(His head bowed.)* —a hopeless final word.

(For a moment Eleanor seems to yearn toward this turmoiling young man.)

ELEANOR. Ha! Would my tongue be wayward too?

(Borden looks eagerly around at her.)

BORDEN. Let it, Eleanor, let it speak for both of us. *(He takes a step toward her.)*

ELEANOR *(Hurriedly.)* Please, John—no! No!

BORDEN *(Angrily.)* This Captain Dare—you love him not.

ELEANOR. It is settled between us. I shall wed him.

BORDEN. For pride and place and family name. *(Bitterly.)* Thus the toil of a man's two hands that would labor for you—counts for naught in this world.

(He strikes his fists together. Sir Walter Raleigh enters from the rear with his hat and cloak.)

RALEIGH *(Warmly.)* Greetings, John Borden.

BORDEN. Sir Walter!

RALEIGH. And you, fair Eleanor.

ELEANOR *(Curtseying.)* Your pleasure, sir.

RALEIGH. What news of Devon, Master Borden?

BORDEN. Four and twenty men are ready to follow you. And there will be others.

RALEIGH. Good! Good! And obedient to orders?

BORDEN. Aye, as independent men should be—no more.

RALEIGH *(Laughing.)* Ah, we Devon folk are all like that. Something in the sea or air that breeds this jealous freedom. But you will sail without me as captain, I fear. *(Eleanor makes a gesture of protest.)* Ah, Mistress Eleanor, I have already read a certain mood in the queen's eye.

BORDEN. Nor shall I sail either, sir. My mother lies a sudden ill.

ELEANOR. John!

BORDEN. On the great book she has pledged me to stay by her till the end. I come to tell you.

RALEIGH *(Staring off.)* You are a dutiful lad, John. 'Tis right.

BORDEN *(Vehemently.)* But someday I'll go—someday.

RALEIGH. Yea, we swear it. You and hundreds more shall go—someday.

ELEANOR. Yes, hundreds!

RALEIGH. Hundreds, say we? Thousands! A mighty stream—men and horses and ships, moving, flowing, toward the setting sun. *(Abruptly.)* But pardon. You know this lady, John?

BORDEN Aye. *(Echoing.)* Lady.

RALEIGH. Fair Eleanor, beauteous and bright, as the rhymesters put it.

(Eleanor curtsies.)

BORDEN *(Turning away.)* Ah, bright. *(With a sharp gesture upward.)* Like that star in heaven there, and no closer.

RALEIGH. You are neighbors, are you not?

ELEANOR. Old friends somewhat.

BORDEN. Aye, somewhat. I am a tenant on her father's farm. I plough his land.

ELEANOR *(Quickly.)* More than that, Sir Walter. He leads the men. They look to him, and—

BORDEN *(He bows.)* Good night, good night to all.

RALEIGH *(Grasping his hand.)* Good night!

BORDEN. Pray command me, Sir Walter, I am your servant. *(He turns and goes quickly off the way he came. Raleigh stands looking after him.)*

RALEIGH. As true a lad as ever bore the queen's arms. True steel, and mettlesome.

ELEANOR. He is!

RALEIGH. And worthy any woman's deep regard. *(Turning to Eleanor.)* Say'st so?

ELEANOR. I would say so if— *(She stares off.)*

RALEIGH. And what is your wish, fair Eleanor?

ELEANOR *(Turning back.)* I wish—I wish that England's ways were different! *(More subdued.)* I mean, Sir Walter, I wish to sail to Roanoke on the next voyage. No more.

RALEIGH. Whether young John Borden goes or not?

ELEANOR *(Quietly.)* I am betrothed, Sir Walter—to Captain Ananias Dare, and together we would sail.

RALEIGH. In spite of every risk you'd go?

ELEANOR. That too!

RALEIGH. Shipwreck perhaps, a watery grave, or missing that, starvation on some lonely strand. Even oaken-hearted men quail before such a voyage.

ELEANOR *(Impetuously.)* And may I go?

RALEIGH. If there were a dozen such women in England!

ELEANOR. I could find you twenty such women in Devon alone.

RALEIGH. Do, and your name will outlast mine. But we waste words.
There may be no colony, men or women. You marked the queen's
attitude. Again and again she denies me leave to go myself to lead
the enterprise, and I fear to trust it to other hands. Aye, refuses even
one shilling's help. "Wait, wait until Spain has had her lesson," she
commands. But our future lies beyond the sea, and every wasted day
cries out its waste.

*(He paces up and down. The milkmaids dance back across the scene and
out at the right to a bright burst of laughter and a roulade in the music.
Behind the stage a great rocket soars up in the sky and breaks in falling
spangles through the night.)*

Look, look! Like that rocket England will perish unless—But why do
you dream of such an undertaking?

ELEANOR. Why does one love when and whom one does? Count one thing
valuable which is another man's bauble? Perhaps through the story of a
poor boy from Devon who later became the great Sir Walter Raleigh—
the fancy caught me, made me think on't and by thinking wove its magic
over me. I only know now day and night I feel this narrow England and
hear the call of the unknown world sounding in my ear. I do, Sir Walter,
like you I do.

(Raleigh nods abstractedly.)

Are not women adventurous like men? Are they not?

RALEIGH. They are, thank God, the best of them.

*(Queen Elizabeth attended by two of her maids-in-waiting comes in at the
rear.)*

ELIZABETH (*As Eleanor curtsies and stands with bowed head.*) La, what a wrecking of times when a queen must run after a man! Come, Sir Walter, is it state matters keeps you here in secret?

RALEIGH. Somewhat of statecraft, your majesty. Question—Shall England be an empire or an island?

ELIZABETH. Uhm. . . . From what I hear of this child she is capable of giving advice on the subject. Well, Sir Walter, while they eat and play the games we must settle your little matter. Now, no growling or chewing the lip behind my back. Rather thanks. You may send your colony to Roanoke.

ELEANOR (*With quick joy.*) Your majesty.

RALEIGH (*Kissing Elizabeth's hand.*) My queen!

ELIZABETH. But you shall not go.

RALEIGH (*After a pause.*) I know. (*Wryly.*) I am reserved for Spain.

ELIZABETH. You are. What think you of Master Ralph Lane to lead the enterprise?

RALEIGH. He is brave enough.

ELIZABETH. And tactful, and of good judgment?

RALEIGH. He is very brave.

ELIZABETH. But bravery most is needed now. Let him set forth next month with some hundred men . . .

RALEIGH. But by your leave I say again—without women there is no stability, no permanence, no home. A hard fact and true, your majesty.

ELEANOR. Yes!

ELIZABETH *(Continuing somewhat sternly.)* With a hundred men! Men who can be spared—to build a fort on Roanoke Island, to lay out roads, plant fields. Some months hence your blessed women can be sent—if you can persuade them to it.

RALEIGH. Your proclamation would persuade them.

ELIZABETH. Tonight I am for play, not argument. *(Gesturing to Eleanor.)* Come, he dreams his empires best along.

(She and her attendants go out at the left. Eleanor starts out after them, turns as if to speak to Sir Walter, but decides not to. She curtsies to him and goes hurriedly away after the queen. Raleigh stands an instant as if in deep thought, snaps his fingers and gazes in the direction the queen has gone. No, he will not follow. He moves up the walkway at the left. The light dies from the center stage and stays dimly on him. Another rocket goes up in the night and bursts in falling spangles and sparkles settling toward the earth. The light follows Raleigh as he moves on. Suddenly, off stage, a great ordnance is shot off. Old Tom who has been sleeping on the ground by a little obscuring bush springs up with a squeal and gazes blearily about him. He tries his empty mug to his lips. The light holds on the little eye-blink scene that follows.)

OLD TOM. Whee-oo, I had a most frightful dream! The world was monstrously overrun by lice with two legs.

RALEIGH *(Who has stopped nearby.)* An apt dream, old man.

OLD TOM *(Jumping around and peering at him.)* Why, 'tis the great Sir Walter communing with his soul!

(Another ordnance is fired off in the distance.)

Lord, they're celebrating you, my lord. *(Fawning toward him.)* Don't you know me, Sir Walter? This is me, thy old neighbor, Tom, down in Budleigh—all set to do thee honor too.

RALEIGH. You've changed since I knew 'ee, Tom.

OLD TOM. Aye, aye. *(Dolorously.)* Sorrow and grief do eat away a man's mortal looks. And you've changed too, Sir Walter. But hearts remain the same, eh, old friend?

RALEIGH *(Handing him a small piece of money.)* Here, get thee something to eat. Eat, not drink, Tom.

OLD TOM. Bless you, bless you. I have a devouring hate of drink. *(He emphasizes his words with his mug, then bethinks himself and snaps it hidingly behind him.)* For drink doth pickle a man's wits, and I who live by me wits can abide no pickling. And mayhap I can do thee a favor sometime, small, pitiful-like though it be. *(He holds the piece of money up between forefinger and thumb meaningfully.)*

RALEIGH. I may need thee, Tom, aye and hundreds more of thy kind. Remember.

OLD TOM. I remember. Whistle but a note of thy great plans and I'll come a-running—crying, a true man, stand and denounce!

(Raleigh moves off into the night. Old Tom looks at the money in his hand and then breaks into a shuffling dance, after which he begins singing and half-chanting.)

A man is down but never out
While he keeps his wits and his friends about,
All evil winds blow some good chance,
Then bury the corpse and keep the dance,
For 'tis, oh, good ale, thou art my darling,
And my joy both night and morning!

(He skips on, shouting.) Landlord! Landlord! *(Waving his mug.)* A mug of Plymouth ale!

(He disappears swiftly toward the tavern. Another cannon sounds off scene at the far left rear, and a shout for Sir Walter goes up from the people there.)

VOICES *(In the distance.)* Sir Walter Raleigh! Sir Walter Raleigh!

(The light dies away from the little scene and rises on the historian who has entered at the right rear.)

HISTORIAN. In the spring of 1585 a colony of a hundred and eight men was sent out from England under the command of Ralph Lane, with John White as artist and Thomas Harriot, the mathematician, as surveyor and historian. White's paintings of life on Roanoke Island are highly valued to this day, and Harriot's report on the plant and animal life found here was the first such study made in North America.

(The historian moves to the left center and stops, the light with him. He continues in his clear and informative manner.)

Lane took possession of the Indian village on the north end of the island where we are gathered tonight. He refortified the place and named it the "Citie of Raleigh." Within a few months the settlement was firmly established and would have survived, no doubt, but for Lane's cruel treatment of the Indians. They rebelled, and he decided to teach them a lesson in authority. One summer night, Lane and his soldiers surprised King Wingina, kinsman of Wanchese, as he rested by his campfire.

(The light dies from the historian and comes up dimly at the far right front as the music begins a low pulse-beat Indian dirge.)

SCENE 5

(Near the edge of the forest, with King Wingina's bark dwelling in the foreground. The front is open to the audience, and the old king is revealed sitting cross-legged in the entrance peacefully smoking his pipe. A few drowsy warriors are sitting around on the ground, armed with bows and spears. Before the king the medicine man, Uppowoc, is performing his rites against the ghosts and devils of the air. He weaves his head about, waves his hands, and chants a sing-song tune. Suddenly the warriors spring to their feet as if feeling some invisible and silent enemy about to set upon them. Uppowoc shakes his head in disapproval, saying all is well. "Way-ye-na-wha-nee!" he declares. Finally they all sit down again, and some of them stretch themselves out on the ground. Uppowoc resumes his supplication once more, throwing

*out his curved hands into the night and pulling them toward him as if draw-
ing peace and quiet into his bosom. Wingina gradually lowers his head on
his breast, and sleep comes over the scene. Uppowoc lies down before him.*

*And now as the music rises in suspended notes, pine branches come moving
slowly and queerly in from the right and left. Behind them the low stooping
forms of Lane and his armed men can be seen. With a wild shriek the medicine man springs to his feet. But it is too late. The soldiers fling down their
pine branches and fly at the Indians with drawn swords and a wild cry of
"Christ our victory!" The medicine man bounds away and disappears into
the darkness, followed by two of the soldiers. Amid the screams and yells of
Indian women in the shadows, the Indians are murdered. In his bark house
the old king stands defiantly up. A soldier emerges from the trees at the rear
and shoots him through the heart. He falls, and Lane and his men gather
briefly about the body, raise their swords and guns in a shout of triumph,
"Victory in Christ!" then dash away.*

*As the dead king lies alone, the medicine man is seen stealing out from the
shadows. He comes slowly and sadly toward the king's body, gazing at it in
desperate fear, as the shrieks of the women subside in the distance into a low
keen. He drops on his knees by his dead king, cradles Wingina's head in his
lap, and calls out "Wingina!" as he cries heartbrokenly, the music crying with
him. The light dies away from him and comes up once more on the historian
who has stepped forward. The music fades out.)*

HISTORIAN. The grieving Indians desperately attacked the colony in an
    effort to avenge their murdered king. Finally Lane grew discouraged
    and decided to abandon the colony. When Sir Francis Drake came by
    in his ships, all hands embarked for England, June 19, 1586. The Citie of
    Raleigh was left deserted. A few days later Sir Richard Grenville arrived
    with bountiful supplies, but too late. He left fifteen brave men to hold
    the fort in the queen's name and sailed for England to report to Raleigh.

    Despite this failure Raleigh persisted in his dream. At great expense
    he got together another colony. And this time it was to be a permanent
    settlement, for it consisted of men, women and children—a hundred
    and nineteen people—who were to build homes in the new world. And
    on May 8, 1587, the last of the expedition assembled at Plymouth ready
    to sail upon the long voyage.

SCENE 6

(The light dies from the historian and comes up on a scene at the right front of the center stage, representing the open yard of a tavern in Plymouth. In the foreground is a table around which several sailors are sitting. They are being intermittently served with mugs of ale by a mop-headed apprentice who appears out of the shadow at the rear. Simon Fernandes, a swarthy middle-aged sea pilot, with a short mean-looking sword hanging from his belt, is standing on the table haranguing a crowd of people—men, women and children. These are members of the colony, assembled with their bundles and pitiful baggage to sail for Roanoke Island. Two soldiers with halberds are keeping order in the queen's name, and another at the right is proudly holding the English flag. As Fernandes carries on his harangue, other colonists come down the walkway at the left front, some of them continuing on their way and out at the right. But most of them stop to hear what is being said. Among the latter is Old Tom, who lifts off his blanket roll and sits down on it fanning himself.)

FERNANDES *(Continuing his tirade.)* Three times I have been pilot on her majesty's ships sailing foreign seas, and three times the merciful Father— *(Lifting his eyes an instant and crossing himself.)* —has seen fit to allow me to return safe home again. I was pilot for his honor, Ralph Lane, on his last expedition to Roanoke. I was pilot before for the brave Captains Amadas and Barlowe, and with Sir Humphrey Gilbert I sailed a thousand miles along that treacherous coast. Can I speak? *(Shouting.)* I ask you!

VOICES. Aye, Simon. Speak it out, Simon. We're listening to ye.

JOHN CAGE. I vouch for ye, Simon. I was with Lane, God forbid.

(One of the half-drunk sailors at the table begins to sing.)

SAILOR.
Oh the stormy winds may blow!
And the raging seas may roar.

FERNANDES *(Roaring at him.)* Belay there, you scupper-wash!

(The sailor lays his head over on the table and is silent. Fernandes goes on more loudly.)

And now I am appointed pilot for this expedition—to Virginia. *(Leering about him.)* How wrong I was to say "aye" to Sir Walter! Such a scurvy mixture of the queen's subjects I never saw before!

OLD TOM *(Calling out.)* We be true men and good as in all England!

VOICES *(Muttering and growling.)* Aye, that we be.

FERNANDES *(More loudly.)* Good men—aye, and half of you lay behind bars for crimes on the queen's highway—till Sir Walter fetched ye out to do his bidding!

A WOMAN'S VOICE. Speak not against Sir Walter.

DAME COLMAN. We owe our freedom to him.

FERNANDES. Freedom? Hah! Freedom, you call it. But wait till the tale is ended. Give over this undertaking, I tell you, give over before it is too late, before you set foot into them three pitiful little ships out there. *(He gestures off toward the right rear.)*

DAME COLMAN. Hah! *(Spits.)*

FERNANDES. If Ralph Lane and more than a hundred strong men failed on Roanoke Island, what do you think will happen to your women and children? And what do you think has already happened to the fifteen men left in that wretched place by Sir Richard Grenville?

OLD TOM *(Half-mockingly.)* What?

FERNANDES *(Venomously.)* I wager I already know. They are dead. The wilderness has swallowed them up as it will swallow you. *(Looking out into the crowd and calling.)* Eigh, John Cage! What say you, John?

CAGE *(An elderly, white-haired man.)* Neighbors, I say it's gospel, every living word. 'Leven months I was there in that cursed land, and I would not go again for all the jewels in Spain. *(Vehemently to a young man who stands at his side with a blanket roll on his shoulder.)* Hearken to me, Tony. Stay here, lad.

(Several other colonists come down the walkway. Some of them have their arms around weeping wives or sweethearts. And one man leads a little boy by the hand. The women hold the men by the arm and they stop. But the man and the little boy go on toward the right rear.)

OLD TOM *(Calling after the man.)* Where are ye hurrying, George Howe?

HOWE *(Stopping an instant.)* The ships are ready to sail, and we should be aboard.

(They go on out at the right. A horn blows a long brazen note from the distance, and some four or five of the younger men turn and hurry away in the direction George Howe has gone.)

FERNANDES *(Calling out as if answering the horn.)* Blow, blow on, old horn of Jericho! Let the walls of the world fall in, but they won't crush me. My luck holds.

DAME COLMAN. Enough—let's be on our way!

FERNANDES. *(Angrily to those about him.)* I tell you, only death awaits you on this mad adventure. Death in that desolate country. Aye, you listen to Mistress Eleanor Dare's talk of freedom and the dream of a new empire. That's the empire you'll get—an empire where King Death sits on the throne. This business is not for your good, nor for the good of England. The queen does not countenance it. Not a penny of crown money goes into it.

(John Borden comes walking rapidly into the scene from the left rear. He stops on the outskirts of the crowd.)

Then who profits by it?

OLD TOM *(Mockingly, as before.)* Who?

FERNANDES *(Looking about him.)* I'll tell you—one man and one alone, Sir Walter Raleigh. All for his honor and glory it is, all to spread his fame across the world. He has no care for you—he has no . . .

BORDEN *(Calling out in a hard cold voice.)* That's a lie, Simon Fernandes!

(Fernandes grips his sword as Borden climbs up on the table.)

VOICES. John Borden! There's a lad, farmer John!

OTHER VOICES. Down with John Borden! Down with Sir Walter!

STILL OTHERS. Shame on ye! Shame!

BORDEN *(Ignoring Fernandes's half-drawn sword as he addresses the people.)* Are we men and women of England or hirelings of Spain?

FERNANDES. Watch your words, Master Borden.

BORDEN. I'm watching 'em, aye, and thee too.

(A few of the colonists who had begun to edge away now return as Borden goes on.)

> Friends, I am nothing but a poor farmer. I have no authority except my own voice. And that I'll use for Mistress Dare and Sir Walter. We have set our faces toward that new world, toward a new life for us all. And are we to be stopped here dulled and dead in our tracks by an old woman's tale of danger and hardship? Then go home, go home now, and the ships waiting out there— *(He gestures off to the right rear.)* — may rot where they lie. Danger and hardship! Aye, the better for it. So we may test the manhood in us, if we be men, if we be women worth the name. Who is this Simon Fernandes that you should listen to him? A Spaniard with a Spanish name mayhap.

(Fernandes suddenly draws his sword, but the two men with halberds spring forward and hold them pointed at his breast. He slowly puts up his blade and steps down from the table.)

Like his master Philip he fears a colony in Virginia. He wishes us to fail. But there will be no failing, not if the sea and the wilderness and all Spain herself conspire against us. No, for blow against blow, we will give them back again.

VOICES. Speak, lad! We'll stand with ye, John!

BORDEN. We have made the cast. We turn our backs upon this little England—to go forth to struggle, to work, to conquer that unknown wilderness—to build a nation there—our nation. *(Lifting his eyes an instant to heaven.)* And with God's help we'll build it.

(Sir Walter Raleigh comes in at the rear.)

RALEIGH. Bravo, John Borden!

(At Raleigh's entrance everybody rises, even the drunken sailors. Raleigh is accompanied by a group of people—the Reverend Master Martin, John White, Eleanor Dare and her husband Ananias Dare, Manteo and Wanchese, and two or three members of the council. With them are two armed soldiers, a drummer and a bearer who carries a coat of arms held high. At their entrance Borden stands embarrassed a moment and then slips quietly down from the table and stands among the crowd. Raleigh, whose tall form towers above the assembly, looks kindly about him. His face marked with emotion, he speaks in a gentle but firm voice.)

Friends, pioneers of a new nation soon to be, I come to you at this parting moment in all humility and pride—humility that to English men and women is granted the privilege of this high endeavor, and pride that you my old neighbors of Devon are to share in it. It is nowise strange that you hesitate at this last moment. For no one can question what it means to take this step. Our good pilot Fernandes here has unrolled his doleful story to your ears, I know.

OLD TOM. Oh, that he has!

RALEIGH. Aye, there are dangers, hardships, unaccountable chances of weal and woe that await you. But that such men and women as you and

John Borden and Mistress Eleanor Dare will win over them I cannot
doubt. As for Fernandes, his bark is worse than his bite. True, he
prefers plundering on the seas to the dull business of colonizing but,
as both the queen and I know, he is the best pilot that sails an English
ship. He will be true to the trust reposed in him and land you safely
in Virginia.

*(He turns and offers his hand to Fernandes who hesitates a moment, takes
it and then hurries away at the right in the direction of the waiting ships.
Raleigh turns and indicates the coat of arms.)*

And herewith as a trust in your permanent planting, this sign and
symbol from her majesty the queen—the coat of arms for the new
Citie of Raleigh in the new world.

(The bearer lifts his standard higher and the people applaud.)

And now to the authority of Governor White and his associate, Master
Ananias Dare, I beg your obedience.

(White reaches and takes the coat of arms proudly.)

Would God that I might sail with them and you, but I am reserved
once more for the wars at home. My heart goes with you, my hopes and
my dreams. God bless you. *(He moves among them embracing them and
shaking hands.)*

VOICES. God bless you, Sir Walter!

JOHN WHITE *(Calling out.)* Lead on to the ships!

OLD TOM. Aye, me hearties, let us go!

*(The colonists pick up their bags and bundles and start across the scene
toward the right rear, led by John White. Manteo and Wanchese touch their
breasts, shake hands with Raleigh, and join the crowd. Raleigh embraces
John Borden and sends him away with a smile. Old Tom now raises a song,
and the crowd joins buoyantly in.)*

COLONISTS.
Oh farewell England, farewell all,
and here's a parting hand.

(Lastly goes Eleanor Dare on the arm of her husband. Raleigh bends and kisses her on the forehead and with tears in his eyes watches her go. As she passes Borden, their eyes meet. She lowers her gaze and moves on. He watches her a moment, then lowers his eyes too. Meanwhile the spirited song has continued, the music accompanying, the flag flying and the drum beating.)

We leave to you our hearth and hall
To seek an unknown land.

(The people are more excited now. At last, at last they are setting forth on the great adventure so long dreamed about. Some of the men wave their hats, and others of the crowd skip and dance along, their voices soaring.)

Oh, the stormy winds may blow
And the raging seas may roar,
But merrily we sail away
To that fair land Virgini-ay-a,
To that fair land Virgini-ay-a!

(Raleigh remains alone in the scene as the people march away at the right. He draws his sword, salutes them with it, and then kneels down with the cross of the sword hilt in front of him in an attitude of prayer. The light dims on him and comes up strongly at the upper right rear, beyond the stage set, disclosing in the distance there the pennanted masts of a ship. As the music continues strongly in the farewell song, the ship starts moving toward the left, beginning its long journey to the new world. The music swells up and dies. The lights fade out.)

INTERMISSION

The Waterside Theatre about 1950, with the control booth at center back, the light towers on either side of the seats, the track on which the ship mast rolls visible just above the waterline, and the fireworks pier at northwest end of the track. (North Carolina Collection, University of North Carolina Library at Chapel Hill)

The Historian in his fancier booth after World War II. (North Carolina Division of Archives and History, Raleigh)

The medicine man, Uppowoc, flings sand and wails as he mourns the death of
King Wingina, killed by the English (act 1, scene 5). (North Carolina Collection,
University of North Carolina Library at Chapel Hill)

At Plymouth before departure, John Borden rallies the colonists to keep up their
courage and go forth to build a nation for the common people (act 1, scene 6).
(North Carolina Collection, University of North Carolina Library at Chapel Hill)

On Roanoke Island women mend a fishing net as the midwife, Dame Colman (in white apron), frets over the birth of Virginia Dare (act 2, scene 2). (Photograph by Aycock Brown; Roanoke Island Historical Association, Manteo.)

Agona offers to relieve Old Tom of his load (act 2, scene 3). (Photograph by Aycock Brown; Institute of Outdoor Drama, University of North Carolina at Chapel Hill)

Father Martin christens the infant Virginia Dare (act 2, scene 3). (Photograph by Aycock Brown; Roanoke Island Historical Association, Manteo)

John Borden and Eleanor Dare at the death of Eleanor's husband, Captain Ananias Dare (act 2, scene 5). (North Carolina Collection, University of North Carolina Library at Chapel Hill)

Old Tom, on guard while the other colonists sleep, realizes, "I who was lately nothing am become somebody. . . . Roanoke, thou hast made a man of me!" (act 2, scene 6). (Institute of Outdoor Drama, University of North Carolina at Chapel Hill)

ACT 2

SCENE 1

(After the intermission, the audience is summoned back to the amphitheatre by a flourish of trumpets. After a pause this is repeated. Presently the house lights die out and the chorus, only dimly seen at the left front, begins a chant, the music accompanying.)

CHORUS.

    We commend to thy almighty protection, thy servants
    For whose preservation upon the great deep
    Our prayers are desired.
    Guard them, we beseech thee, from the dangers of the sea,
    From sickness and death,
    And from every evil.
    Conduct them in safety
    To the haven where they would be.—Amen.

(As the chorus chants, a great shaft of light comes up back of the main structure of the center stage, and the tall masts of the ship can be seen in its rays, moving from left to right like something in a dream. The shaft of light dies out, and the lights come up on the chorus as its chant strengthens.)

    God is our hope and strength, a very present help in trouble.
    Therefore will we not fear, though the earth be moved,
    And though the hills be carried into the midst of the sea;
    Though the waters thereof rage and swell,
    And though the mountains shake at the tempest of the same.
    Be still then and know that I am God.
    I will be exalted among the nations
    And I will be exalted in the earth.

(The light fades from the chorus and rises on the historian who is standing at left center stage.)

HISTORIAN. After a long and stormy voyage the colony arrived at Roanoke Island on July 23, 1587. Landing parties were at once sent out for the relief of the fifteen men who had been left behind the year before. The party with John Borden and Captain Dare was the first to reach the fort.

(The light dies from the historian and comes in full on the center stage, revealing the interior of the fort as Lane and others had built it. At the center back is a little chapel, topped by a cross, and with the wrecked interior open to the audience. To the left of that is a little cabin and to the right another little cabin. Jutting in from either side at the front are the roof edges of still other cabins. A few boxes, casks and bales are scattered about, rude furniture overturned, and in general the scene shows signs of having been recently plundered. And now the sound of an English snare drum is heard coming in at the right. Ananias Dare enters at the head of some eight or ten armed men—John Borden, Manteo and Wanchese among them. At a gesture from Dare, the small cortege stops, grounds arms and looks curiously about, and the flag bearer rests the butt of the flag staff against the earth. The drum is silent.)

DARE *(Calling loudly.)* Hooah! Show yourselves! Heeoh—friends!

(At another gesture from him, the drummer drums a tattoo beat. Presently from the direction of the woods at the right front a voice is heard calling.)

VOICE. Yona—yona—ee—yay-Wankees!

(Wanchese looks up from the center stage, listens a moment, and then hurries over to the front of the scene and stops. Outlined against the darkness of the forest at the right the figure of Uppowoc, the medicine man, can be seen. The call is repeated.)

UPPOWOC. Yona-yona, Wankees!

(Wanchese suddenly runs out from the center stage, and passing by the fringe of the audience, leaps up the steps and onto the bank at right. Uppowoc bows before him. Suddenly Wanchese grabs him by the arm.)

WANCHESE. Mish-wi aga, Wingina?

UPPOWOC. Ne bah na-tee-o, Wingina.

DARE *(Calling out loudly on the center stage.)* Form fours! *(The soldiers straighten up and arrange themselves in a stiff military posture.)* What news of the fifteen men, Chief Wanchese?

WANCHESE *(Lifting his right hand, palm outward, as he answers.)* I am no longer a chief. I am the king now. *(With an ironic salaam.)* I must go to my people. *(He turns and disappears into the forest with the medicine man.)*

BORDEN. Stop him, Captain Dare! Stop him! *(He starts forward. Dare throws up his hand.)*

DARE *(In a prim schoolmasterish manner.)* Soldier John Borden, once more I command you to your place—in the ranks. If the noble Indian has traffic with his people in the forest, we have no right to stop him. *(Borden starts to reply, then bows his head and resumes his place.)* We will now advance to the end of the island in search of our friends.

BORDEN. What think you of the fifteen men, Chief Manteo?

MANTEO *(Gravely.)* The white men may be dead—gone. *(He gestures toward the sky.)* Come.

DARE. Advance at guard!

(The drummer begins to beat his drum again, and they march out at the left, the flag going gaily before. They have hardly disappeared when a voice is heard calling off at the right.)

VOICE. Wait, comrades, wait for me!

(Old Tom comes puffing in, his doublet undone, and his ancient musket hanging loosely in the crook of his arm. He stops and stares off at the left.)

OLD TOM. Leave me, do they, all in the heat of their youth and great marching, and me with the weight of years upon me back. Across this wild territory they tear, like their hose were girt with garters of fire, and me hacked and slashed to bits with a power of thorns and godless briars! (*He sinks down on a box and wipes his hot face with his sleeve, after which he looks curiously about him.*) Ah, I could do with a mug of Plymouth ale!—Bah!—What a wilderness and desolation! So this is Roanoke Island in the new world, this is the land of Sir Walter's great visioning and Mistress Dare's wise words of encouragement. What a woman, and she to be the mother of a new babe in two weeks or three! Ah, poor babe. (*Rocking from side to side.*) Heave, ship, blow storm, and always the same. We are sailing to the new land of freedom, we are pioneers of a dream, me hearties. Ah, well, the blind man eats many a fly. (*Spitting and half-singing.*) O the stormy winds may blow, and the raging seas— (*With a sickened shudder.*) Urck! Eight weeks shut up in the belly of that little ship—and me swearing a great oath on the mercy seat of God—Give me dry land again and I would be Christian flesh from then on. Well, this is dry land—but nothing more. (*He lifts a handful of sand and lets it trickle through his fingers, then climbs wearily to his feet.*) Ah, how green the grass grows in England! And I could already wish me back there tasting of good mutton on the Devon hills. (*He walks gingerly about the scene, peering into the cabins and pushing over boxes. Suddenly he grips his gun and whirls about as if he felt an enemy creeping up on him from behind. He breaks into a laugh.*) Hah-hah-hah, what a fool I am! (*Looking off at the left again and calling.*) Captain Dare, Captain Ana-ni-as Dare! Where is every soul? (*Striking his breast.*) Peace, you organ of wind! After all they are near at hand, and Governor White is approaching. I am sworn to bravery and great endeavor. Sir Walter depends on me. Then he shall hear of my deport— (*His voice dies out with a gasp and he stands staring at the cabin to the right front. He begins to shake like a man with a chill. With a loud cry, he tears out at the left, calling as he goes.*) Help! Help! (*At the same moment voices are heard hallooing off at the right.*)

VOICES. Heigh-ya! Hoo-ee!

(*Immediately John White, with Simon Fernandes, Reverend Martin and soldiers, enters. Old Tom re-enters and runs up to John White.*)

OLD TOM. Master White, good Governor White, look, look!

(He points to the cabin at the right. White, Fernandes and the soldiers hurry over to the cabin, stand a moment in silence, then turn back toward the center of the stage.)

A SOLDIER. One of our countrymen.

WHITE. He has been dead very long. *(Shaking his head.)* The Indian method—they broke his bones.

FERNANDES. As they will yours and your followers'.

WHITE. Peace! *(Looking off at the left and shaking his head.)* Look ye, how bravely my son Captain Dare marches. The Indians could ambush the whole of them.

FERNANDES. And they will.

(A murmur arises among the men.)

WHITE. Rest.

(They drop down and squat about on the ground. Dare comes in with his little group of men, drum, flag and all. Accompanying Manteo now are his little son Wano and his wife Meeta. She is weeping with happiness as she clings to his arm.)

DARE. Halt! *(His troop stops, and he salutes Governor White.)* We have sorrowful tidings, sir, from Manteo's wife.

MANTEO. *(Indicating his wife.)* She saw men from Wanchese's tribe come and kill the white men during the last moon—some drowned, all of them are dead.

(White stands with his head bowed in thought.)

FERNANDES *(Satirically.)* Shall we unload the women from the ships, Governor? They are over-weary in their cramped quarters.

WHITE. First we must remove the dead. Borden, take three soldiers. *(Borden and three soldiers go off into the shadows at the right rear. White turns to the others.)* Later we will inter the broken body decently. *(To the group.)* We have arrived too late to aid those brave men who held this fort in the queen's name. But thankful still we are to Almighty God that he in his kindness has brought us safely to our new home.

(He gestures to Reverend Martin who goes up to the front of the little chapel and lifts his hands in prayer. Governor White, Captain Dare and all the soldiers pull off their caps and fall on their knees.)

REVEREND MARTIN.
Almighty God, our Father, we thank thee for thy mercy and
    compassion upon us.
Yea, in thy great wisdom thou hast seen fit to bring us safely to this
    haven—
Here thou hast commanded us to build our homes and a temple to
    thy name—
Thou hast given us this land to have and to hold forever to thy great
    honor.
We have it not by our own sword, neither was it our arm that gat it—
But thy right hand, and thy arm and the grace of thy favor
That vouchsafed it unto us.

(John Borden and the three soldiers come quietly in and bow down with the others.)

And in the thanksgiving of this hour
Let us remember in sorrow these thy servants
Who perished here before, a sacrifice
That we the living
Might continue in their stead.
Above their ruined and scattered bones
We swear devotion to our cause.
And not unto us, O Lord, not unto us
But unto thy name be given the glory.
Amen.

(They all bend and kiss the earth, then rise to their feet.)

WHITE. And in the spirit of this prayer I command you to go in peace amongst our enemies. Let there be no efforts for revenge against the Indians. At Sir Walter's express charge we are to foster friendship with them. I counsel ye, make no untoward move against them on pain of grievous punishment.

(Borden and his three companions turn around and then begin moving backward across the scene, holding their muskets at the ready. The other soldiers move over to the left and stand with their weapons ready, for Wanchese, accompanied by Uppowoc and three warriors with spears and bows, comes out of the woods at the right front. He carries a long-handled flint-headed spear. The medicine man shakes his rattle menacingly and warningly. The soldiers are on the alert at seeing Wanchese.)

DARE. *(Somewhat excitedly.)* See ye—it's Wanchese! Wanchese!

WHITE. We greet you again, Chief Wanchese. What do you wish?

WANCHESE. *(In a hard cold voice.)* You white people must go. You must leave our land now.

DARE *(With sudden authority.)* Disperse at once. We order it in the queen's name and Sir Walter Raleigh's.

OLD TOM *(Emboldened as he holds his musket before him.)* Get out of here, ye knavish rogues! Scat!

(Wanchese suddenly makes a guttural growl and a move at him, and Old Tom springs back with a squeal of terror.)

WANCHESE *(In the same dull hard voice.)* You white people must go. Leave!.

WHITE. Come now, come. This is our land. Captains Philip Amadas and Arthur Barlowe made treaty for it, and in England we swore eternal friendship to her majesty the queen—Chief Manteo here and you.

WANCHESE. Chief Manteo is a snake.

(*Manteo starts forward, and the warriors around Wanchese lift their bows. The soldiers raise their muskets likewise. Manteo stops and stands looking at the ground, his whole form trembling.*)

WHITE (*Shouting.*) Ground arms!

DARE. Ground arms, men, ground 'em!

(*The men slowly lower their guns.*)

WHITE (*To Wanchese.*) Put down your weapons. We come as brothers.

WANCHESE. I have no brother. Wingina was my brother and you white men killed him. This I shall never forget. Upon the full moon every white person will be gone. If not— (*He draws his hand across his throat, then hurls his spear before him. It sticks quivering in the earth a few feet in front of Manteo. Wanchese turns and strides back into the forest, Uppowoc and the warriors accompanying him.*)

OLD TOM. Mary in heaven, I feel the knife at me throat!

WHITE (*After a pause.*) An idle threat. What say you, Chief Manteo?

MANTEO. My people will make a great fight with Wanchese! We will kill him! Kill him! (*He jerks the spear from the ground and breaks it across his lifted thigh, then flings the pieces from him.*)

WHITE. With Manteo as our ally we have no fear. His tribe is powerful. (*Looking at Fernandes.*) What do you advise, Simon Fernandes?

FERNANDES (*Still sarcastically.*) I am a pilot. I brought you safe across the sea. Unload my ships and I will sail again to England.

WHITE. Sir Walter advised we settle farther north if we found conditions bad here. What do you advise to that?

FERNANDES. I advise nothing.

WHITE *(Turning to the men.)* Soldiers, men, it is set down in our articles of government that we hear opinions from you all. And 'tis right, for in the building of a country, men must act together or that country will fail. You have marked the tragedy here, you have seen this sudden threat of Wanchese. You know the report of Master Lane. Shall we abide here or sail on and plant a new colony on the Chesapeake? What say you, Master Dare?

DARE *(Looking about him.)* There are arguments on both sides.

WHITE *(Grimacing.)* G-o-o-d! *(To George Howe.)* Sergeant Howe?

HOWE. I like not this place.

WHITE. Soldier Borden?

BORDEN. First I do stand ready to maintain as ever that Simon Fernandes is no friend of this colony.

WHITE *(As always, anxious for peace.)* Now, now, John Borden—

(Eleanor Dare comes in at the right rear, accompanied by Dame Colman, the midwife, and two colony soldiers. She is very pregnant.)

BORDEN *(Not perceiving her.)* Did he not lewdly forsake our flyboat in the Bay of Portugal?

FERNANDES. Proof—proof, I challenge you!

ELEANOR *(Calling out.)* Proof or not, it's true! We all saw it!

(At her words they all wheel around and Governor White hurries over to her.)

WHITE *(In alarm.)* My child, we left you resting in the boat!

ELEANOR *(Smiling.)* Think you I'd remain there quietly waiting— waiting? See, I am well attended. *(To Borden.)* What is this quarrel with Fernandes?

BORDEN *(Bowing, and with a touch of coldness.)* Fernandes refuses to carry us farther north. *(Addressing White and the others again.)* And why? Because it is his desire that we remain here to be destroyed as others have been before us. He fears the new settlement on the deep waters of the Chesapeake as a threat to Spain. *(In a huff Fernandes storms off in the direction of the ships.)* Let him fear. But I say this is the better site even so. For there we needs must start a new settlement, shelter and fields to be made. Here we have them already. There we would be at the mercy of the Spanish pirates in their big ships. Here the shallow sounds protect us. There the winters are fierce, here they are mild. Let us dare Simon Fernandes's advice and remain here.

VOICES *(From the soldiers.)* Aye, we agree.

ELEANOR. Well spoken, John Borden.

WHITE. That it is—well spoken. Mount the guard!

HOWE. Mount the guard.

DARE. Sergeant Howe, keep a watchful eye. But no display of firearms, we command you.

(The men scatter around, some of them take their places at the right and left, and others go up on the walkway at the left and stand on watch. Borden takes the flag from the bearer and mounts aloft behind the little chapel. Old Tom steps savagely out into the center of the stage and aims his musket in the direction Wanchese has gone.)

OLD TOM. Old Beelzebub Wanchese, show but a horn and I'll shoot it off for ye. Oh, but I will, Mistress Eleanor. *(Shaking his fist toward the right.)* This is our country now, and we be ready to defend it till Gabriel blows his judgment horn. Did not another man slay his thousand with the jawbone of an ass? Eigh, then what a mighty destruction of lives I could manage with this weapon of terror! I am good for a whole army of Indians.

DAME COLMAN *(Pointing toward the rear.)* The flag, the flag!

(A cheer bursts from the men, and they twirl their caps in the air as Borden fastens the flag above the stockade. The music begins playing a dynamic martial air—the powerful notes pouring across the scene and echoing through the dark forest. The cheering of the men dies out, and Borden speaks above the swelling music, his voice fresh and triumphant.)

BORDEN. Three cheers for our new home—Virginia!

WHITE. Three cheers!

ALL. Hooray! 'Ray! 'Ray!

ELEANOR. And may this flag never fall except as we fall first! Long live
    Virginia!

ALL *(Cheering.)* Virgini-ay! Virgini-ay!

(The music makes a strong salute and dies. White calls out loudly through the scene:)

WHITE. Unload the ships!

DARE. Unload the ships!

(Dame Colman and the two soldiers solicitously attend Eleanor back the way she came. Borden hurries out at the right rear to assist in the unloading. The music strikes up in the dynamic old ballad of "Sir Walter Raleigh's Ship," and the colonists, men and women, now begin entering from the right and right rear, fetching household belongings—bundles, bags, hampers, etc. One man carries a spinning wheel and another a cradle. Here follows a choreographed action of getting settled—cleaning up the debris of the fort's wreckage and setting things to rights. White and Dare participate in the action somewhat as overseers, pointing and helping. All sing as they work, the pantomime fitting the rhythm of the song.)

COLONISTS.
    Sir Walter Raleigh's ship went a-sailing on the sea,
    And her name it was the name of the Golden Trin-i-tee,

As she sailed upon the lone and the lonesome low,
As she sailed upon the lonesome sea.

*(Some of the women are now busy in the chapel, pushing the pulpit back
into place and the little baptismal font likewise. Others are cleaning out the
cabins. The historian stands at the left front observing the work.)*

There was another ship went a-sailing on the sea,
And her name it was the name of the Spanish Rob-ber-ee,
And she sailed upon the lone and the lonesome sea,
As she sailed upon the lonesome sea.

*(Still other colonists have entered, Borden and Old Tom among them.
They join in the action.)*

Up stepped a little lad, Great Sir Walter, Lord, he said,
What will you give to me if I sink her down like lead,
If I sink her in the lone and the lonesome low,
If I sink her in the lonesome sea?

Ten thousand pounds in gold shall be given unto thee,
And unto my daughter fair likewise wedded you shall be,
If you sink her in the lone and the lonesome sea,
If you sink her in the lonesome sea.

*(The scene fades out, and the light holds on the historian. The music reprises
a bit of the ballad and dies.)*

HISTORIAN. The colonists settled in and around the fort. The chapel was
restored, buildings were repaired, fields chopped and ploughed, and
roads cleared. A smithy and weaving room were soon set up, and in a
few days Fort Raleigh looked like a thriving permanent settlement.

(The light fades from the historian and comes up on the center stage.)

SCENE 2

(At the downstage center several of the colony women have spread a great fish net on the ground and are beginning to mend it. Two sentinels pace back and forth along the high parapet built across the palisades. The flag still flies in its place as before. The women are singing as they work.)

WOMEN.

Adam lay ybounden,
Bounden in a bond;
Four thousand winter
Thought he not too long.

And all was for an apple,
An apple that he took,
As clerkes finden written
In their book.

(Dame Colman, the midwife, comes hurriedly in from the right and crosses the scene over toward the cabin at the left front. She is a spry peppery little woman of about fifty, with a kerchief tied over her graying hair. Joyce Archard, a youthful woman of about thirty, calls out to her.)

JOYCE. How fares it with Mistress Dare, Dame Colman? *(But the midwife has already gone into the cabin.)*

ELIZABETH GLANE *(Another of the group, about twenty-five.)* I hope it will be a boy.

ALICE CHAPMAN *(About twenty, slow of speech and with a bit of a stutter.)* And I—I would a—they—they named him Walter Raleigh Dare.

MARGERY HARVIE *(About thirty, a motherly sweet woman.)* Aye, it would please Sir Walter, proud and great though he be in England.

JANE JONES *(A tired-looking young woman of about twenty-five.)* And how would he be hearing of it across the great water? *(Murmuring and staring off.)* The great water.

JOYCE *(With firm energy.)* Now none of that, Jane Jones. This is Virginia.

MARGARET LAWRENCE *(A vivacious girl, about seventeen or eighteen.)* Governor White will carry news when he sails.

JANE. When he sails. Every day draws nearer toward the time of storms. And we need supplies.

JOYCE. This is no time to talk of supplies and we on Roanoke Island only two weeks.

JANE *(As the midwife comes out of the cabin at the left with some linen and a basin.)* I dreamed last night Simon Fernandes weighed anchor and fled away to England leaving us to die.

JOYCE. Whist on your dream.

DAME COLMAN *(Locking the cabin door with a great key and coming forward.)* And I wish he might sail away and the governor with him. Here they sit around waiting—waiting in a clutter. I have delivered a hundred strapping Devon girls in my time, yea, and more, and I don't need their help here.

JOYCE. Is everything well?

DAME COLMAN. Is everything well? You'd think never had a babe been born into the world before. Lah, but then it's Mistress Dare who is the mother and sure she is greater than the Virgin Mary.

JANE. Oh, you shouldn't talk so.

DAME COLMAN. No? Wait till you hear me railly talk. And if they don't get some of the crowd away from my door I'll begin. There sits Master Dare and the Reverend Master Martin on a cushion of pins. And the blessed governor, anxious grandfather, with his brushes ready to paint the portrait the minute the wee girl comes into the world.

JOYCE *(Laughing.)* Girl?—But we are praying it will be a boy.

DAME COLMAN. Well, it won't be, for I can't abide men.

JOYCE. But without men your job would be lost.

DAME COLMAN. Then I would mend fish nets with you. And now won't you tell me why these same men don't catch any fish with all them mighty nets you're fixing?

JOYCE. Because Wanchese's tribe has got possession of the fishing grounds, that's why.

DAME COLMAN. And why haven't we got possession of the fishing grounds?

JOYCE. There's to be no bloodshed. The governor's orders—and wise ones too.

DAME COLMAN. They're all cowards. Only one man among them—John Borden. Without him and the help of Manteo, God bless that savage, this colony would not last a six month. *(Old Tom comes in at the left with two buckets of water hung from a yoke over his shoulder.)* Oh, there you are!

(She darts over to him, dips out a basin of water and hurries away at the right. Old Tom starts on heavily. An Indian woman comes in, following along close behind him.)

OLD TOM *(As the women begin to laugh.)* Laugh! Laugh! Here I am a beast of burden and all me valor perished in me feet. *(Turning angrily around on the Indian woman.)* Leave me in peace, will you? Be scarce and get gone. Phewt! *(But the Indian woman only smiles at him, and the women laugh again.)* Funny, ain't it? But there's scripture for me condition. Didn't they set Sampson to grind in a mill? Yea, and what did Sampson do? Wham, and down came the great pillars!

JOYCE. It's your lady-love we're laughing at, Tom, not you. Oh, but she's faithful.

OLD TOM. Aye, since the day she heard me singing down by the creek, I won her savage heart away. *(Yelling.)* Scat, you old—old sow! Whew, she's all anointed with bear grease again! Love ointment it is, people.

JOYCE. You should be proud to be so sought for.

OLD TOM. Ah, Lord, what a wonder is this? Here I went years and years in England without so much as a glimpse of a woman's sweet favor, and now I'm favored to undoing! *(Yelling.)* Get out! Trot, run, march! *(But the Indian woman only smiles the more blissfully at him.)* Verily this is a new land of opportunity, as Mistress Dare maintains. Oohm, me a ladies' man and nothing but a water-carrier to the fields.

JOYCE. How is the work going there?

OLD TOM. Worse and worse, which is to say more and more. John Borden is a demon for labor. The men all grumble and growl, but he laughs and sings. And water—water—water. Well, well, well, when the springs of the world run dry I shall rest.

(Far in the distance a faint call of "Water, water" is heard. Old Tom starts hurriedly off up the walkway at the left, calling as he goes.)

Coming, coming, Master Borden!

(He waddles on and out, the Indian woman padding softly after him. The women watch them go, and then Joyce begins to hum in a rich contralto voice. They all start singing again.)

WOMEN.
Ne had the apple taken been,
The apple taken been,
Ne had never our lady
A-been heaven's queen.

Blessed be the time
That apple taken was.
Therefore we moun singen
Deo gracias!

(A group of little boys, some five or six, of different ages, ranging from six to fourteen, come scurrying in down the walkway at the left front. They variously carry rude fishing poles, a string of fish or two, bundles of sassafras roots, and flowers. Two men with muskets accompany them to the center stage and leave when the boys are safely with the women. The little boys show the women their possessions.)

THOMAS ARCHARD *(About eight years old.)* Look, Mother, the fish we ketched. Manteo showed us where to find them.

GEORGE HOWE, JR. *(About ten years old.)* And see the sassafras roots. They will make good tea for father's fever.

THOMAS SMART *(About nine.)* I got some flowers for the baby. Has God sent it yet?

JOYCE. God is sending the baby now.

THOMAS SMART. But he is so slow.

JOYCE. You boys run along. Master Bennett is waiting with the catechism.

WILLIAM WYTHERS *(About thirteen, scowling.)* I thought we wouldn't have school today.

JOYCE. Run along.—And give the fish to the cooks.

(The boys go out at the right. Manteo enters at the left. At the same time John Borden comes rapidly down the walkway at the right front. He is stained with sweat and dust from laboring in the fields. Behind him are three or four young men, likewise toil-worn and begrimed. They carry shovels and a mattock.)

BORDEN. Is the net finished?

JOYCE. It will do.

BORDEN. Good. Greetings to you, Manteo. *(Manteo bows, and Borden turns to the women again.)* Take the net down to the boat. Tony Cage swears to a great run of fish around the point. *(The women rise, fold the net and carry it out at the right. Borden now speaks strongly to the men.)* There is yet two hours of sun for working in the fields, men. I will come later. *(The men go out at the left.)* Is there still no news of Wanchese?

MANTEO *(Shaking his head.)* He hides in the forest.

BORDEN. He may, but his men don't. Again last night they raided our fields, tore up our nets and tried to fire Master Dutton's house.

MANTEO. Too many of your men go out alone. They must go together.

BORDEN. That is the order, but some of them won't obey. George Howe is down the shore fishing now. I warned him.

MANTEO. There is great danger. Tell Governor White what I say.

BORDEN. I will, but I tell him the same thing.

(Manteo bows and goes back the way he came. Two artisans enter at the right, one rolling a wheelbarrow and the other carrying a grubbing hoe. They stop by Borden.)

FIRST ARTISAN *(As Borden examines the wheelbarrow.)* A monstrous fine piece of handiwork—if I did construct it.

BORDEN. But you should've made the wheel out of gum. It's tougher.

FIRST ARTISAN. There ain't no pleasing you, Sergeant.

BORDEN. Not till it's done right.

(The man rolls the wheelbarrow off.)

SECOND ARTISAN. Sergeant, us have the medicine now to cure them grass and roots. *(With a proud chopping motion.)*—Hah—

BORDEN *(Examining the hoe.)* Good—good. We want a score of them, come Monday a week. Forks too.

SECOND ARTISAN. You'll have 'em, sir, trust me.

(He goes out. Old Tom comes tearing in from the right and runs to the farm bell by the little chapel and begins ringing it violently.)

OLD TOM *(Calling out above his loud ringing.)* Hear ye—hear one and all!

(Borden turns quickly around, hurries to the right and looks off and then comes back into the scene.)

BORDEN. How is she—Mistress Dare? *(Loudly.)* Speak, man.

OLD TOM *(As the colonists begin to enter from the right and left.)* Oyez! Oyez! Hear ye! Hear ye! This the eighteenth day of August, fifteen hundred and eighty-seven, a daughter is born to our beloved Mistress Eleanor Dare! Oh yes! Oh yes!

(John White, Captain Dare and Reverend Martin come in from the right. By this time a crowd has gathered jubilantly in front of the chapel. Reverend Martin enters there and stands above the people. The troops of little boys rush in pell-mell, and behind them the Indian woman. She sees Old Tom and pushes her way through to be near him. He looks at her, suddenly stops ringing the bell, throws up his hands and stands near Reverend Martin as if for protection. Manteo and a few of his warriors enter from the left and stand on the outer edge of the crowd.)

REVEREND MARTIN *(As the people bow down on their knees, Manteo and his family doing likewise.)* O Lord, save this woman, thy servant.

PEOPLE *(In a chanted response.)* Which putteth her trust in thee.

REVEREND MARTIN. Be thou to her a strong tower.

PEOPLE. From the face of her enemy.

REVEREND MARTIN. Lord, hear our prayer.

PEOPLE. And let our cry come unto thee.

REVEREND MARTIN. O Almighty God, which hast delivered our beloved Eleanor Dare and thy servant from the great pain and peril of childbirth, grant, we beseech thee . . .

(Suddenly the sentinel on the high outlook at the left rear lets out a great cry.)

SENTINEL. Indians! They're killing Master Howe!

(He lifts his gun and fires. Manteo springs away to the right, followed by his men. Borden runs with them. In the distance wild yelling is heard. The women and children begin to wail and cry as they gather beseechingly around their minister in the chapel. The light blacks out on the center stage and rises on the historian at the left front.)

HISTORIAN. A day later three other settlers were ambushed and killed— Tony Cage, William Clement and Thomas Ellis—as they were cutting reeds to thatch their cabins. The colonists buried their dead and went determinedly on. Manteo met the savages in a pitched battle and drove them over to the mainland. Governor White set a price on the head of Wanchese and made Manteo lord of Dasamongueponke and all the surrounding country and subject under him to Sir Walter and the queen.* On August the thirteenth Manteo had been baptized as a Christian and on Sunday the twenty-fourth the new baby was christened.

SCENE 3

(The light fades from the historian and rises on the center stage. The colonists are gathered in and before the chapel. Near the altar and rude font within are Reverend Martin, Dame Colman, Joyce Archard, John White, Ananias Dare and John Borden. On the rear wall above the altar is a large framed painting of the Virgin Mary. At the right front of the crowd outside are Old Tom and near him the Indian woman. Over at the left front the end of a table projects into the scene. It is loaded with a keg of ale, fruits and provisions. And to the rear of it are Manteo, his wife and son and a group of his warriors. Simon

*Editor's note: The sentence incorporates language from John White's diary. Dasamongueponke was an Indian village across from Roanoke Island on the mainland at a site near the present location of Manns Harbor.

Fernandes and two or three of his sailors are near them looking on. As the lights go up, the music begins playing a traditional hymn tune, and the colonists sing.)

COLONISTS.

With thankful hearts, O gentle Lord,
We bow to thee in one accord,
Obedient to thy kind decree,
"Let little children come to me."

Once long ago our Saviour's word
The children of Judea heard,
Soft answer to their lowly plea—
"Come, little children, come to me."
Amen.

(The song ends, the light comes up more brightly within the little chapel, and Reverend Martin begins the baptismal ceremony.)

REVEREND MARTIN *(Holding the new baby aloft, a little bundle of white.)* Dearly beloved, in as much as our Heavenly Father has seen fit to bless us with this child, thereby sending us a token of his favor and marking this settlement with the sign of permanence, we do return thanks for his bounty and mercy. *(Some of the little boys inside pop up for a better view of the baby but are pulled down instantly by their elders beside them.)* Conscious we are of this great event—to be marked and set down in history for all time to come. *(His voice strong and sonorous.)* This the first English child to be born in the new world! *(He turns to Borden and Joyce.)* And now the godparents, John Borden and Joyce Archard, chosen of the church— *(Pausing.)* —name this child.

JOYCE. Virginia.

BORDEN. In honor of this our country.

REVEREND MARTIN *(Dipping his hand into the font and sprinkling Virginia's forehead.)* I baptize thee, Virginia, in the name of the Father and of the Son and of the Holy Ghost, Amen. *(He makes the sign of the cross on her brow.)*

PEOPLE. Amen.

REVEREND MARTIN. The Lord be with you.

PEOPLE. And with thy spirit.

(The music sounds a salute, and the people all come out of the chapel. Old Tom begins to ring the bell, and the four musicians who have been standing among the crowd with their lutes, viol and tabor seat themselves on some boxes at the right and fall to tuning their instruments. Two or three others begin drawing ale from the keg and passing it out in mugs, first to Governor White and those near him. The Indian woman gets hold of a mug and takes it over to Old Tom. He drops his bell-rope, gives her a wink and a smile and takes it. Dame Colman, the midwife, comes down out of the chapel with little Virginia Dare, and immediately there is a great pushing and crowding around to get a look at the baby. The dame allows them this favor a brief moment and then takes her precious charge away at the right, some of the little boys tagging along behind and pulling at her apron.

And now the musicians strike up an English country dance. The men and women pair off, and the governor dances with Joyce Archard. Finally Old Tom and the Indian woman are going it along with the rest, and even Manteo gets out into the scene for a few turns with his wife. As the dance continues, Fernandes lifts his head and is seen scanning the heavens. He speaks to the sailors and they go out at the right. The dance ends, the dancers applaud, and then Governor White climbs up on a box. With a mug of ale he gestures to those around him.)

VOICES. Speech! Speech!

GOVERNOR WHITE *(As the crowd grows silent.)* Friends, this is a happy day for us. It marks the permanent beginning of English colonization in the new world. Blest of God and his holy church, our colony will from this day forth go on to a greater destiny. The hour has come at last when I must sail again to England. But I go happily in the knowledge that I leave behind me here a contented settlement. *(There are murmurings of agreement from the people.)* And now I do declare that by your vote duly recorded in the book of colony affairs—this Citie of

Raleigh in Virginia and the lands adjacent thereto are placed under the joint rule of Captain Dare, Eleanor Dare and John Borden—Captain!

(Dare, surprised and angry at Borden's promotion, stalks off. Not heeding Dare, the rest applaud. Voices break out.)

VOICES. 'Ray!

OTHER VOICES. Borden! Borden! Captain Borden!

STILL OTHER VOICES. Speech! Speech !

BORDEN *(Embarrassed, he speaks simply.)* Till you return, sir, we shall be true to our trust.

VOICES *(White and the others are caught short by Borden's lack of words this one time, but after a moment cheering breaks out again.)* Yea! 'Ray for Captain Borden!

(Borden steps back.)

GOVERNOR WHITE. And now farewell. Before the coming of Christmas you shall see us again with several shiploads of provisions, other men and women and children, our neighbors, to add to our number. Mayhap this time the Queen will relent and Sir Walter himself will accompany me back. *(The crowd applauds.)* God be with you.

PEOPLE *(Fervently.)* God be with you, Governor White!

(White starts away at the right, Captain Borden following him. The music begins softly playing, and the crowd goes solemnly after them. Old Tom comes along with his yoke and buckets as the last of the people leave. The faithful Indian woman is still behind him. She taps him gently on the shoulder indicating that she will willingly carry the burden. He stares at her in joyful astonishment and gleefully puts down the yoke. Tenderly she places a necklace over his head and adjusts it on his shoulders and chest. As she moves off to the left with the yoke, he skips joyously behind her. He bursts into happy song, the music accompanying.)

OLD TOM *(Singing.)*
O once I was courted by a lady of color,
I loved her I vow and protest,
I loved her so well and so very well
That I built me a bow'r in her breast, in her breast,
That I built me a bow'r in her breast.

(He gives her an affectionate pat.) Lead on, me honey, you have won
me manly heart away. *(She goes on out at the left, Old Tom following
behind.)*

Oh, up on the mountain and down in the valley,
I tell the glad news all around—

*(Now the people, standing along the ramparts at the rear and off scene, burst
into cheers for the departing Governor White. The great shaft of light comes
up once more behind the palisaded fort at the extreme right, and the masts
of White's ship can be seen, moving back to the left, headed home. The men
and women cheer and wave their kerchiefs, and the music builds toward a
climax of salutation. The illuminated masts of the ships disappear at the left,
the shaft of light dies, the music sinks down to silence, and the light comes up
once more on the historian now at the right front.)*

HISTORIAN. But John White's voyage home was beset with violent
storms, and only after great hardship and suffering did he finally reach
England—November 5. By the next spring, 1588, when he had secured
ships and supplies, all thought of colony or empire across the sea
had dropped from the queen's intent. For now Philip of Spain was
preparing his great armada against her, and all resources were called
upon for defense.

SCENE 4

*(The light dies from the historian and comes up in a strong concentration
at the left front, revealing a corner of the queen's council chamber. Queen
Elizabeth is revealed sitting in a lofty throne-like chair, the members of her
privy council behind her, and Sir Walter Raleigh standing to the right and
before her. Just behind Raleigh is John White, leaning on a stick, his head*

bowed. Lord Essex, a proud and dominant man, is standing behind the queen. The queen is talking violently and angrily.)

ELIZABETH. How many times do I have to tell you no! No, no, I say again! *(Reaching her arms up pleadingly in the air.)* This Raleigh will have the very heart out of me with his colony. *(Wagging her head.)* Night and day he pursues me, sends messages to my door, haunts me in my dreams with "Roanoke, Roanoke! My people are perishing in yonder world!" 'Fore God in heaven, I should clap him in a dungeon and hush his clamor. And that I will—I will if he persists. O Essex!

ESSEX *(Touching her shoulder comfortingly.)* Patience, dear queen, you fret yourself for naught.

ELIZABETH. "Dear queen"—ah, that it might ever be so with you all.— And he knows I cannot spare him for a prison, not while Philip threatens me. No, that I cannot. And so he presumes upon me. *(Her voice dies out and she stares at Raleigh.)* Speak—speak, will you?

RALEIGH *(Bowing.)* If I may.

ELIZABETH. "If I may"—always that knife of courtesy to cut my kindness in two—you—you— *(Half-breaking down.)* I shall never understand you.

RALEIGH. It is but a simple thing I request, your majesty, to save my colony in Virginia.

ELIZABETH. Simple—hah? Like the breaking of a neck. And do you think I'll risk my country's neck by allowing you to leave England? *(Rising quickly.)* Did I not warn you! *(Clapping her hands and calling loudly.)* The guard!

ESSEX. Pray, your majesty—

ELIZABETH *(Bitterly.)* Queen, queen—majesty—majesty! *(Almost glaring at Raleigh.)* You'd think I'm but a scullery maid to cleanse the kitchens of my people for all you hearken to me. *(She sinks down in her chair and buries her face in her hands.)*

RALEIGH *(Quietly.)* Your majesty, I must give over to your wish. I do not go to Roanoke, so be it. But pray listen to this my pleading.

ELIZABETH. Once more—and yet once more. Then speak—there was a phrase I used once—aye, you strange and proud and dreaming man.

RALEIGH *(Bowing again.)* Out of your great right, pray call me what you will. But no one less than a queen would doubt my loyalty to England.

ELIZABETH. Nor does your queen doubt it, Sir Walter.

RALEIGH. Then count me brave and let them write me down brave fool in ages yet to be.

ELIZABETH. Leave that to history to decide between us two. Your request?

RALEIGH. I have through several devious ways arranged for funds—to purchase two small ships.

ELIZABETH. And you would send them to your colony.

RALEIGH. At once—with provisions. God knows how stands it with them there!

ELIZABETH. You know my orders of these several months?

RALEIGH. I do—no ships may leave these shores.

ELIZABETH *(Trying to control her anger.)* Yes.

RALEIGH. But then I begged a fleet of ships before. And these are only two and small at that. They could be spared, with Master White.

WHITE *(Coming forward and bowing down on his knees.)* Your majesty, I beg you. My daughter—her baby—day and night they call to me. *(Brokenly.)* I cannot endure it. Let me go to them.

ELIZABETH *(Loudly.)* Rise, Master White. *(He climbs tremblingly to his feet.)* There is an old saying taught me by my nurse—a little thread can often save the rope from breaking. Perhaps these tiny ships might be the holding strand against the King of Spain. *(After a dramatic pause.)* But I consent.

WHITE *(Bowing up and down abjectly.)* Your gracious majesty and queen beyond compare—your holy grace—they will be saved—be saved!

ELIZABETH. Yet if Philip attacks us and we lose— *(Looking sternly at Raleigh.)* —then for this tiny thread, these little ships that might have turned the tide, Sir Walter shall pay forfeit with his head.

(A trumpet sounds in the music and the queen rises quickly as a messenger enters. Falling on his knees, the messenger presents a letter which Elizabeth takes and tears open. She reads it and then smiles strangely at Sir Walter.)

It seems that destiny doth make the choice. Between my England and your Virginia, it favors me. Would God it did not in such a tragic way as this. *(Loudly.)* In this hour no ships shall leave England, large or small. For by the sea we live. To lose it is to perish. Gentlemen, a Spanish armada is set to sail against us. And now to arms—God save us!

(Again a flourish, deeper-toned and more ominous this time, sounds in the music. Consternation runs among the group. Essex grabs the queen's hand, kisses it and strides away at the left. The queen and the others hurry out. Raleigh and White are left behind.)

WHITE *(In a low agonized voice.)* This means the end of the colony. It will die.

RALEIGH *(Staring before him.)* As many of us shall—that England may live.

(He goes slowly away at the rear, White following like a broken man. Far in the distance a high, strident and summoning trumpet is blown. The scene fades out and the light rises once more on the historian now standing in the walkway.)

HISTORIAN. And so all resources of England were kept for defense against Spain. And on Roanoke Island the colonists waited with sickened hearts for the help that never came. Day after day, night after night, month after month, they watched and worked and waited. But never the white sail of a ship was seen, never the mariner's cheer was heard to tell that help was nigh. Only the murmur of the vast and sheeted waters or the sad whispering of the dark forest broke upon their uneasy dreams.

SCENE 5

(The light fades away from the historian. The music begins a slow dead march, and a dim glow rises on the center stage and suffuses the scene. A funeral cortege is seen entering from the right led by Eleanor Dare with a book held before her. She is reading a funeral service. John Borden walks by her side. Four men carrying a rude coffin follow behind, accompanied by Joyce Archard and several women and children who are weeping silently.)

ELEANOR *(The music softly accompanying.)*
  I know that my redeemer liveth,
  And that I shall rise out of the earth in the last day,
  And shall be covered again with my skin,
  And shall see God in my flesh,
  Yea, and I myself shall behold him,
  Not with other but with these same eyes.
  The Lord giveth and the Lord taketh away,
  Even as it pleaseth the Lord
  So cometh things to pass.
  Blessed be the name of the Lord.

MOURNERS. Blessed be the name of the Lord.

(The funeral procession passes on out at the left. Eleanor's voice fades away in the distance, and the light dies. The music holds a long and apprehensive note and then is suddenly shocked with an anguished cry of its own, a cry of warning. Somewhere in the darkness a single woman's scream is heard, and then another from the sleeping stockade around. Yells go up in the night. A surging spotlight hits the right front of the stage. The figure of Wanchese is seen creeping forward there, followed by several of his warriors. Colonist women, led by Eleanor Dare, are now fleeing across the scene and taking refuge in the chapel. Wanchese and his men spring forward to attack the

frightened women. John Borden and several of the colonist men rush in from the left rear and meet them in the center. A hand-to-hand struggle follows. Shots and screams fill the air. The fury of the music increases. The light surges in and out on the fight. We hear old Tom yell on his parapet walk aloft. The spotlight illuminates him briefly there as he clubs at the head of an Indian who is trying to scale the palisades from the back. Dame Colman has scurried up the ladder at the right rear and she and Joyce Archard with brooms and clubs are seen fighting at the climbing Indians as the spotlight hits them for an instant. The light surges in at the left front and Manteo comes flying in with a few of his warriors.)

DAME COLMAN *(Crying out from the parapet.)* Manteo's come!

VOICES. Manteo! Manteo!

(A fire breaks out by the cabin at the left front. Several of the colonists— women and children—spring forward, beat at the fire, throw sand on it and put it out. The spotlight now hits Captain Dare hurrying in with his men from the left front—as if arriving from an outpost.)

Captain Dare!

OTHER VOICES. Captain Dare! 'Ray! 'Ray!

(A few of the fighters have fallen wounded and dead in the background. Captain Dare and Manteo drive Wanchese and his few remaining warriors out at the right front, pursuing them off. Smoke is now rolling across the scene, the flashes of musket fire have continued and the battle score has thundered its way in the music. The battle dies down. The music holds its long lengthened note again. The women huddle moaning in the chapel. We see Captain Dare in the spotlight at the right front now staggering back into the scene, an arrow in his back. He wavers along by the right front cabin clutching at the logs for support.)

A WOMAN'S VOICE *(Crying out.)* Captain Dare!

(He plunges to the ground, face downward. Eleanor runs forward and kneels by him with a cry. She stares in horror at the arrow and holds the dying man to her. Borden hurries forward out of the shadows at the left.)

BORDEN. Captain Dare. Captain Dare! *(He kneels down.)*

ELEANOR *(After a pause.)* He is dead.

(The light fades from the scene and comes up on the historian at the left.)

HISTORIAN. The Indians were driven off in defeat, but at a heavy loss.
Wanchese was slain as Manteo had sworn. Manteo himself was badly
wounded. And along with Captain Dare several colonists were killed,
among them Henry Johnson, Humphrey Newton, John Starte, Martin
Sutton, Clement Taylor and Ambrose Viccars. The government of
the colony now devolved upon Eleanor Dare and John Borden. With
unflagging spirits they strove to supply food, keep up the morale of the
settlers and take care of the ailing. And every day the whisper ran—
"Food will come before the summer ends. Surely before the season of
storms Sir Walter will send his ships." But summer came and went—
then autumn. And the specter of starvation faced them on their second
Christmas.

SCENE 6

*(The light dies on the historian and comes up inside the cabin at the right of
the chapel revealing Eleanor Dare sitting by a cradle in which Virginia Dare
is sleeping. She is singing a lullaby, and her fingers fly back and forth weaving
a rush basket as she sings. In the center of the scene at the front is a large iron
pot with a circle of dull red coals under it. On the parapet at the back the dim
figure of the sentinel can be seen as he keeps his watch. It is early evening of a
winter day.)*

ELEANOR.
When Jesus came from heaven
To be a little child,
He chose a lowly maiden,
His mother, Mary mild.
To warm him were the oxen,
His bed a manger bare,
And for our needs he suffered
Great want and cold and care.

The Waterside Theatre after the 1997–98 renovation, with the control booth center back, a smaller seating area with armchair seats, riprap at water's edge beneath the track for the mast, and the fireworks pier moved to southeast end of the track. (Photograph by Michael Booher; Roanoke Island Historical Association, Manteo)

Prologue, with the cast ranged across the stage for choral speaking (act 1, scene 1). (Photograph by Michael Booher; Roanoke Island Historical Association, Manteo)

Sir Walter Raleigh presents Wanchese and Manteo to Queen Elizabeth (act 1, scene 4). (Photograph by Michael Booher; Roanoke Island Historical Association, Manteo)

Challenged by Manteo, Wanchese (on crate) demands that the colonists leave Roanoke Island and return to England (act 2, scene 1). (Photograph by Michael Booher; Roanoke Island Historical Association, Manteo)

Agona offers to relieve Old Tom of his load (act 2, scene 3). (Photograph by Ray Matthews; Roanoke Island Historical Association, Manteo)

Sir Walter Raleigh pleads with Queen Elizabeth to allow aid for the Roanoke colony (act 2, scene 4). (Photograph by Ray Matthews; Roanoke Island Historical Association, Manteo)

The colonists leave Fort Raleigh on their final march into the wilderness and out of recorded history (act 2, scene 6). (Institute of Outdoor Drama, University of North Carolina at Chapel Hill)

(Somewhere in the distance at the rear the muffled sobs of a woman are heard. Eleanor listens a moment with strained attention and then resumes her singing.)

    Lord Jesus, now from heaven
    Where thou art Lord of all,
    O send thy blessed angels
    To guard this baby small.
    For peace in dark and danger
    Thy loving-kindness brings.
    O bend above, enfolding,
    The shadow of thy wings.

(A low call of "Eleanor" is heard in the cabin at the left of the chapel. Eleanor rises, takes up a mug and comes out to the pot. She dips the mug in and goes to the cabin at the left. As she enters, the light comes up on the interior revealing the wasted form of the Reverend Martin as he lies propped up in his rude bed. At the same time the light dies away in the cabin at the right.)

ELEANOR *(Putting the cup to the sick man's lips.)* Drink, Father Martin, you will feel better.

REVEREND MARTIN *(He makes an effort to drink and then pushes the mug away and smiles weakly at her. In a tired desolate voice which he tries to make cheery:)* Thank you, my child.

ELEANOR *(Tidying the bed a bit.)* Now you sleep and rest. We'll have some good potato soup in a little while.

REVEREND MARTIN. Any news from John Borden?

ELEANOR. It's a long way from Hatorask, but he will be here soon now— soon.

REVEREND MARTIN. Aye, that he will. *(The woman's low sobs are heard again in the distance.)* And God grant that he bring you good news. *(Listening.)* Is that Sister Margery?

ELEANOR. Yes.

REVEREND MARTIN. She loved her baby. The Lord giveth and the Lord taketh away.

ELEANOR *(Recitingly.)* Blessed be the name of the Lord.

REVEREND MARTIN *(After a moment.)* Eleanor, I have had a strange dream. I saw a great swan—white and with wings like a ship and it was flying south. *(Sighing and closing his eyes.)* Flying south it was, through the still blue sky, and I could feel the breath of air from its wings against my cheeks, and the air was warm—it was warm. And out of its mouth came melodious words sweet as an angel in paradise and it was saying, "Follow me, follow me." I wonder was it a sign?

ELEANOR. What sign, Father?

REVEREND MARTIN. To leave this spot. *(As she stares at him.)* Evil has been wrought here, the spilling of blood, the murder of innocent ones. Shall we ever thrive here? Mayhap that was a voice sent from God to warn us to leave this place.

ELEANOR. No! No! *(Dropping down on a rough stool and gazing before her.)* But sometimes I think— *(Then shaking her head firmly.)* No, we must bide here. *(Rising in a sudden show of cheerfulness.)* This is the better place. The Indians no longer molest us. Sixty of us still remain alive and spring will soon be coming. We have our houses, and in April we will plant crops. It was only a dream.

REVEREND MARTIN. It is ninety days till April.

ELEANOR. John Borden will never desert the fort.

REVEREND MARTIN. And you will stay with John Borden.

ELEANOR. I will.

REVEREND MARTIN. And in the spring you will be wed.

ELEANOR. Aye, Father, in the spring.

REVEREND MARTIN. God's blessings on you two and on us all, my child.

ELEANOR. Amen.

REVEREND MARTIN. And how does little Virginia?

ELEANOR *(Sitting down again.)* She is so pitiful and so thin. But in her sleep she smiles so—so—she does— *(She suddenly bows, gripping her knees.)*

REVEREND MARTIN *(Lifting his hand to rest on her head.)* Grieve not, my child. Somehow we shall win. I have God's promise—in my heart I have it.

(The light fades down in the cabin and comes up on the center stage emphasizing the pot. The Indian woman comes in at the right front, bowed under a great bundle of firewood. Old Tom follows behind carrying a tow-like bag in his hand.)

OLD TOM. Sweet my love, unload. *(He helps her lift off the wood.)* Whew, but an ox could carry no more. Eigh, I am the most fortunate of men. *(Eleanor comes out of the cabin.)* How fares it with his reverence, Mistress Dare?

ELEANOR. He is sleeping now.

OLD TOM *(As the Indian woman squats down and begins to tend the fire.)* I have a bit of business with him when he mends— *(Gesturing.)* —her and me. Brr-rr, but it's cold. Stir up, Agona, stir up.

ELEANOR. Agona?

OLD TOM. I have lately christened her Agona—which is to say in the Indian tongue—"Agony." Brr-rr—but I've been sleeping cold of nights. *(He bends over, sniffs the pot, and puts his hand affectionately on Agona's head.)* Hmm, I never knew a stew of leaves and stale corn to smell so good.

ELEANOR. Drink Tom. The children have eaten. But save something for Master Borden.

(She hands him the mug and he dips it into the pot. He starts to raise it to his lips, then hands it to the Indian woman. She gives an appreciative smile, drinks, and hands it back to him. Eleanor pulls her shawl about her and goes up into the little chapel.)

OLD TOM *(Calling out.)* I have four more berry candles for the altar. Agona made 'em.

(He takes the candles from the bag and goes up into the chapel. The music begins a Christmas carol. The candles are now lighted inside the chapel, revealing the snow-white altar around which Eleanor and old Tom are working. Bits of holly and mistletoe hang from the beams above, and the picture of the Virgin looks sweetly down upon the scene. Now in the distance at the left front the sound of singing is heard—a mixture of children's, women's and men's voices.)

ELEANOR. They're coming—with the yule log!

OLD TOM. And may our hearts keep as warm as the fire it makes.

(He and Eleanor come out of the chapel and move over toward the left to meet the oncoming singers. Two small sickly boys enter from the left, down the walkway, carrying tapers and leading the yule log procession. Immediately behind them a group of ragged young men come carrying a large log about six or eight feet long, and behind them the rest of the colonists—men, women and children. Some of them carry tapers, others little bunches of holly or bits of ground ivy. They all are dressed in nondescript clothes, old capes, shawls, and pieces of blankets, skins and woven stuffs. They are singing a Christmas carol as they enter. Eleanor moves down and steps between the two little boys, taking them by the hand and leading the procession with them. As the log-bearers reach the pot they place the log next to the fire, and the procession moves on in a circle around the pot. At the right some of the more elderly and feeble of the colonists creep in to join as best they can in the pitiful festivities— among them Margery Harvie supported by the almost tottering Dame Colman. The song continues as the procession moves on in the circle.)

PEOPLE *(Singing, the music accompanying.)*
   Nowell, Nowell, Nowell,
   Nowell, Nowell, Nowell, Nowell.

This is the salutation of the Angel Gabriel.
Tidings true there become new,
Sent from the Trinity
By Gabriel to Nazareth,
City of Galilee.
A clean maiden and pure virgin,
Through her humility,
Hath conceived the person
Second in Deity.

OLD TOM (*Shouting above the singing.*) Hurrah for old yule!

PEOPLE (*Still singing.*)
Hail, virgin celestial,
The meekest that ever was!
Hail, temple of the Deity!
Hail, mirror of all grace!

(*As the procession passes around the pot again, Eleanor moves up into the chapel. The people crowd toward her and stand looking into the chapel, singing. The candles are now extinguished, and the light widens on the scene.*)

PEOPLE.
Hail, virgin pure! I thee insure,
Within a little space,
Thou shalt conceive, and Him receive
That shall bring great solace.

(*The song and music die, and they all kneel down on the ground for a moment of silent prayer. Eleanor then rises and goes up to the altar. The people still kneel beggingly and piteously where they are. She opens her prayer book and reads strongly and comfortingly.*)

ELEANOR.
The Lord is my light and my salvation—
Whom shall I fear?
The Lord is the strength of my life—
Of whom shall I be afraid?

(Low moans of pain and hunger and grief begin to break among the people.)

> For in the time of trouble
> He shall hide me in his pavilion,
> Yea, in the secret places of his dwelling
> Shall he hide me,
> He shall set me up upon a rock.

(The little bleating cries and calls grow more insistent and louder among the people.)

> Hearken unto my voice, Oh Lord,
> When I cry unto thee.
> Have mercy upon me and hear me!
> Oh, hide not thy face from me,
> Nor cast thy servant away in displeasure.
> Have mercy upon us,
> Oh Lord, have mercy!

A CHILD'S VOICE *(Plaintive and high.)* I'm hungry, mommee!

(The low lamentation of the people now seems stimulated by the child's call, and the pleadings grow louder. A woman breaks into sudden and shrill hysterical sobs. Another woman's voice rises in a dolorous lament.)

WOMAN'S VOICE.
> O Death!
> O Death rock me asleep!
> Bring me to quiet rest,
> Let pass my weary guiltless life
> Out of my careful breast.

(Other voices are added in a hoarse muffled harmony.)

> Toll on the passing bell,
> Ring out my doleful knell,
> Let fly sound, my death tell.
> Death doth draw near me.

There is no remedy, no remedy,
There is no remedy.

(The sentinel on the parapet lets out a high wild cry.)

SENTINEL. Merciful God! Merciful God, save us! Save us! *(He flings up his arms and lets his gun fall. Then he jumps headlong down into the scene and bobs his head about in prayer. The cry runs among the people.)*

VOICES. Save us! Save us or we perish! O God have mercy upon us!

(A few more of the women grow hysterical, the children begin to cry, and three or four men outside the chapel fall to beating their breasts in a paroxysm of woe. Eleanor springs up and moves among the women trying to quiet them. Joyce Archard does likewise. The men continue to moan and pray. Eleanor comes down out of the chapel.)

ELEANOR. For shame—shame! You frighten these little children. Are ye men or cowards? *(She seizes the sentinel by the collar and tries to shake him.)* Stop it! Stop it!

(John Borden, accompanied by three raggle-taggle soldiers, comes suddenly down the walkway at the left.)

BORDEN *(His words cutting across the scene in a loud command.)* Silence! *(Snatching a gun from the nearest soldier, he fires it into the air. The hysteria subsides. The colonists hurry toward Borden, some still jerking and shivering and others emitting low moans. Borden strides over to the sentinel and pulls him to his feet.)* Back to your post!

SENTINEL *(Beating his hands together.)* I cannot, I cannot. Ten hours I have stood the watch—ten hours and I am perished with cold! *(He staggers and falls.)*

BORDEN. Take him to his bed. *(Two soldiers come over and lift the sentinel up. Borden takes a mug from Old Tom, dips it into the pot and gives it to one of the soldiers.)* Make him drink of it. *(They bear the sentinel away.)*

A VOICE. What news, Master Borden?

OTHER VOICES *(Rising in vehemence.)* Yes—tell us! What news?

BORDEN. Friends, there is news, but it must wait.

(A growling murmur goes up from the colonists.)

VOICES *(Bitter and jeering.)* Wait! Wait!

OTHER VOICES. Tell us now!

BORDEN. I command you to your cabins. Get yourselves rest, and tomorrow the council will be called.

VOICES. Tomorrow! Down with John Borden! Aye, down with him!

(The Reverend Martin comes creeping in from the left rear. He stops and stands holding to the corner of the chapel for support.)

REVEREND MARTIN. Blessings, my children.

(Jubilation breaks out among the colonists, and some of them run to him and kiss his hands.)

VOICES. Father Martin! He is well again. Thank God, thank God!

REVEREND MARTIN. Yes, yes—I have had a sign from God—of white swans on the move. His words came to me—a voice speaking—saying fear not, all will be well. Go now and sleep. Go. *(With benign authority.)* Go to your beds!

(Quieted by his gentle voice, they all gradually move out of the scene at the right and left. Old Tom stops by the Indian woman who has already stretched herself out on the ground.)

OLD TOM *(Pulling her up.)* Come to your bed, old lady.

(He goes out with her at the left. Eleanor moves over to Reverend Martin.)

ELEANOR. You must lie down now.

BORDEN. Good night, Father.

REVEREND MARTIN. Bless thee, my lad. On thee we rest. *(He takes Borden's hand and joins it with Eleanor's, then lifts his own in blessing over them.)* In you two—united—the symbol of our strength shall remain secure. God bless you. Good night.

(Eleanor goes with Reverend Martin into the shadow at the left rear. Borden stands by the pot, his head bowed in thought. Then looking about him, he spies the sentinel's gun, picks it up and returns with it to the fire. He satisfies himself that it is primed, lays it aside and begins holding first one foot to the coals and then the other, his shaggy stern face lighted by the dull glow from below. Eleanor comes quietly back and stands by the fire opposite him. He looks at her, smiles, and then brings a box forward for her to sit on.)

BORDEN. He is very ill.

ELEANOR. Yes.

BORDEN. And in his fever—dreams of signs and wonders and hears the voice of God.

ELEANOR. Would that the others could hear the same if it gave them peace. And you? Sit down and rest.

BORDEN. Even if I would, my feet keep on walking from habit—and my arms, rowing, rowing.

ELEANOR. And now tell me—the news is bad.

BORDEN. Yes. *(Eleanor bows her head.)* Manteo is dead.

ELEANOR. I feared it.

BORDEN *(Speaking swiftly.)* The tribe—what is left of them—is in despair. Tomorrow they begin moving south back to their home in Croatoan. The game has fled away from these islands, food is scarce. A few pitiful

bushels of corn they had, no more. They could spare none, nor pota-
toes. On Croatoan there will be game. *(He begins pacing back and forth
by the fire.)*

ELEANOR. If the ships do not come soon—tomorrow—

BORDEN They will not come—neither tomorrow nor the next day. I know
it now.

ELEANOR *(Quietly.)* And how do you know it?

BORDEN. Rowing the sounds and tramping those endless bogs and
wilderness of salt sea grass, my mind worked in a turmoil of fever and
fret. Why? Why? Why? I kept asking myself—why has no sign, no word
come from the governor and Sir Walter? What could keep them back?
Suddenly I saw the answer. How, I know not, but the answer came.
England is at war with Spain.

ELEANOR *(Springing up.)* It's true. We should have thought of that.

BORDEN. And the queen keeps back all ships for her defense.

ELEANOR. And may for months to come. Now we must act. Thank God
for that. We have supplies in the storehouse to last us but two days at
most.

BORDEN. And what would you do?

ELEANOR. If there is game farther south, then we must find it.

BORDEN. And desert the fort?

ELEANOR *(Sitting quietly down again.)* My mind runs fast ahead. *(Looking
up at him.)* Only if you wish it.

BORDEN. If I wish it. *(Smiling down at her, the hardness of his face softening
away.)* Thus we agree—we two, standing here tonight upon the outpost
of the world, the last survivors—keepers of a dream.

ELEANOR *(Murmuring.)* A dream!

BORDEN. And we'll keep that dream—keep it to the end!

ELEANOR. Yes, we will—together we will.

BORDEN. Together—aye, that's it—together—we two. *(Eleanor bows her head. His voice rises with a touch of fervor.)* All this hardship, this desolation and death sit lightly upon me when I think of you. To fight for you, to work for you till I fall in my tracks—that is enough. *(He lays his hand on her shoulder.)*

ELEANOR *(Reaching up and taking his hand.)* Think not of me but of the others. *(She puts his hand against her cheek.)*

BORDEN. That too— *(Looking up into the night.)* And by that great spirit that guards this world and holds our little lives in the hollow of his hand I swear we will fight on and on here until this wilderness is won.

ELEANOR *(Murmuring.)* And you will win.

BORDEN. Even if we die, we win. For— *(Vehemently.)* Ah, Eleanor, tonight I feel—somehow it was meant to be this way. Somehow a destiny, a purpose moving deeper than we know has brought us both together here upon this lonely land—to prove our love, to test our strength— aye, to make us worthy of the heritage we hold for those that shall come after us. For as we hold true— *(He bends and kisses her on the forehead and then stands up straight, his voice filling with a firmer strength and certainty as she rises and clings to him.)* And if in the wisdom of God we should be forced to live out our days here forgot and deserted of the world, I should have no regret—none.

ELEANOR *(After a moment—lifting her head bravely.)* Nor I.

BORDEN *(Staring ahead of him, his voice running on as if in communion with some listener in the dark.)* No regret—none. Yea, once Sir Walter said—the victory lieth in the struggle, not the city won. To all free men it standeth so, he said. Out of his suffering he knew. *(He kisses her and*

holds her close to him.) And so we know—tonight we know. And down
the centuries that wait ahead there'll be some whisper of our name—
some mention and devotion to the dream that brought us here. Ah—

*(His voice dies out. For an instant they cling together. Off at the right rear
a woman's voice is heard singing. Margery Harvie enters half-clothed and
walking like one in a dream.)*

MARGERY *(Her hands held before her as she sings.)*
Sir Walter Raleigh's ship went a-sailing on the sea,
And her name it was the name of the Golden Trinitee,
As she sailed upon the lone and the lonesome low—

BORDEN *(Hurrying over to her, he tries to lead her back the way she came.)*
Come, Margery, you must bide in your bed.

MARGERY. The ship—Sir Walter's ship. Look, there it goes.

*(She breaks away from him. Eleanor goes to her and puts her arm around
her.)*

ELEANOR. This is Eleanor, Margery.

MARGERY.
There was another ship went a-sailing on the sea,
And her name it was the name—

JOYCE *(Running in from the rear with a blanket, she wraps it around
Margery.)* I dozed a bit, and then she was gone.

MARGERY *(Crying out.)* My baby! My baby! Oh, Queen Elizabeth!

JOYCE *(Leading her off.)* Darling, we'll find him, yes—yes, we will.

*(They go out at the rear. Borden stands a moment watching them, then turns
and takes Eleanor by the arm.)*

BORDEN. And you must rest too. Come.

ELEANOR *(Her body shaken as if with an ague.)* Take them away from here, John! Take them away! They can stand no more! They are dying—all of us are dying here.

BORDEN *(After a moment of silence.)* I know—I know—you must sleep now. Tomorrow—tomorrow—we shall—

ELEANOR. Yesterday—today, all day they kept coming to me, begging me to let them leave this place. Let them go. Promise me. *(She suddenly pulls his head down and kisses him vehemently.)*

BORDEN *(With resolve.)* Tomorrow we will all decide. *(Loudly.)* But the Citie of Raleigh shall not die!

ELEANOR *(Leaning heavily on him.)* Not while we live.

(He leads her into the shadow toward the cabin at the right rear. Old Tom enters at the left with his musket. Looking about him, he clambers up the ladder at the rear and places himself on watch on the parapet, taking the place of the sentinel. Borden reenters.)

BORDEN *(Hoarsely.)* Come down from there, Tom. It's my watch.

OLD TOM. You're dead on your feet, John Borden, and here I am all in the prime of a great fervor. *(Borden who is staggering with weakness, turns toward the fire and sinks down on the box.)* Agona snores like a hundred horns in bedlam. I can't sleep.

BORDEN *(Groggily.)* Can't sleep—say you can't sleep? Hah-hah-hah.

OLD TOM. But you can. And while I walk this post with me instrument of vengeance you'll all be safe as Peter's rock. *(Authoritatively.)* Lie down, lie down, young man, and ease your weary bones.

BORDEN. With men like you, Tom, we'll win this fight.

OLD TOM. I am your man, Captain Borden, small and pitiful-like though I be.

(Borden leans over from the box, topples down on the ground and lies sprawled out by the fire.)

BORDEN *(Calling drowsily.)* Thank 'ee, Tom, thank' ee. You will be remembered.

(He sleeps. Old Tom begins walking his post, the light emphasizing him a bit.)

OLD TOM *(Talking to himself.)* I will be remembered. I hope not. *(Stopping and staring through the night.)* There in England all remembered me— aye, with kicks and curses and a terrible usage of tongues they did. Hah-hah-hah. And deep I drowned me sorrows in the mug. But here where there is no remembrance I who was lately nothing am become somebody. For, item—have I not now the keeping of some sixty souls in me care—I who could never care for me own? Verily, Tom, I hardly know thee in thy greatness. *(Saluting the air.)* Roanoke, thou hast made a man of me!

(He draws himself up and marches proudly back and forth a few times. But gradually his steps slow, and finally he leans against the palisade and remains motionless as he gazes off into the darkness. The music begins to play a low requiem as if addressed to the scene. Borden stirs restlessly in his sleep, and Old Tom's head is seen sagging over on his breast as if, for all his great endeavor, weariness were overcoming him. The light dims slowly down. For a moment the music continues. Suddenly off at the left a man's voice is heard in a high halloo. Old Tom jerks his head up, looks about him, and hurries over to the extreme left of the parapet. Then he lets out a loud challenge.)

OLD TOM. Who comes there! Halt in the queen's name!

(He raises his musket as one of the colonist runners comes flying in at the left, his gun dragging in his hand and his clothes in tatters.)

RUNNER *(Calling.)* Captain Borden!

OLD TOM. Stop your yowling. Let him sleep.

RUNNER. Captain Borden!

BORDEN (*Raising his head as the light brightens on him and the center stage.*) Who calls? (*Springing to his feet as the runner hurries over to him.*) What is it?

RUNNER. Rouse the people! A Spanish ship has anchored in the inlet.

BORDEN (*Seizing him by the arm.*) Are ye certain?

RUNNER. Aye, sir, by their flags and colors—a ship of war. They bespoke me in their broken tongue.

BORDEN. I fear Fernandes has betrayed us.

RUNNER. Nay, I know not. A party came ashore. They send us terms. Surrender peaceful, we will be protected—and fed.

OLD TOM (*From above.*) We'll not surrender! We'll fight to the last man, Captain Borden!

RUNNER. If we resist we are to be killed—to the last man— (*Gasping.*) — and woman and child. (*Beseechingly.*) Oh, Captain Borden, they will murder us! They will!

(*He falls exhausted on the ground. Borden springs away to the bell and begins to ring it loudly.*)

OLD TOM (*Shouting down from his walkway.*) Assemble, assemble! Everybody assemble!

(*Eleanor Dare comes out of her cabin. Borden is seen gesturing and speaking to her. She hurries away at the right. The colonists begin to run into the scene from the right and left—men, women and children—in their pitiful clothing. A medley of excited voices breaks around Borden.*)

VOICES. What is it? Have the ships come? They've come! They've come! Sir Walter's ships! Oh, thanks unto God!

(*Some of the men and women begin to embrace one another in trembling jubilancy. Borden stops ringing the bell and stands on the steps of the little chapel. By this time other colonists have assembled. They all grow silent waiting for him to speak.)*

BORDEN. Friends, I fear the hour has come when we must leave the fort. But you shall decide—whether we stay or whether we go—

VOICES *(Bursting out in a high pleading.)* What is it, John Borden? Speak, speak.

BORDEN. We must decide—the fate of this colony.

BENNETT *(A stalwart, lean-faced young man.)* The fate of the colony? What do you mean?

BORDEN. Decide—whether we leave this fort, or whether we stay.

VOICES *(Bursting out in a high agonized pleading.)* Speak, Captain Borden, tell us!

PEOPLE. Yes, what is it?

BORDEN *(Lifting his hand as the colonists keep crowding around.)* Manteo's people are moving south where there is game. They offer us haven with them.

A WOMAN'S VOICE. But why wake us from our sleep to tell us that?

OTHER VOICES. Aye—and ring the bell—like the murdering Indians were on us again. Yea, and all hell screaming in our ears.

PEOPLE *(Wildly.)* Yes, why?

BORDEN *(With a shout.)* Because the time is urgent!

(The runner staggers to his feet.)

RUNNER *(Loudly.)* Friends, a Spanish ship has anchored off the bar.

(A pall of horror falls upon the assemblage and they stare at one another with stark faces.)

VOICES *(Whispering.)* The Spaniards! The Spaniards!

(Bennett throws out his hands in a great gesture.)

BENNETT. The treason of Simon Fernandes has borne its fruit.

BORDEN. Mayhap, Mark Bennett, it is so.

RUNNER. They have a man-of war to destroy us. Tomorrow or the next day they will reach here and attack us. We are too weak to stand against them. Too weak.

(He moves over to one side, and a number of the colonists immediately begin gathering around him.)

ELIZABETH GLANE *(In a high frightened whimper.)* Let us leave this cursed place.

JOYCE ARCHARD *(Wrapping her arms around the hysterical girl, hugging her to her.)* Shame on ye, Elizabeth, shame!

(Dame Colman and Eleanor move among the women and ragged children, trying to quiet them.)

RUNNER *(To the group around him, fiercely.)* I tell ye the Spanish offer us terms. *(Gesturing off at the left.)* A party awaits our surrender there. We have but to show a white flag. They will spare our lives.

VOICES. Surrender, surrender!

(At a push from the runner, a youth darts into one of the cabins.)

OTHER VOICES. Stay here and we shall be slaughtered in cold blood. Leave! Leave! Leave!

BENNETT. Silence!

(The runner lifts his hands to cry out again. Bennett rushes toward him as if to knock him down and silence him, but a number of colonists surround the runner to protect him.)

VOICES. Let him speak!

(Hysteria is beginning to run among the people.)

BORDEN *(Above the turmoil.)* Let us behave ourselves like soldiers!

OLD TOM *(From the parapet.)* Aye, that we will, Captain Borden!

(But still others gather around the runner, some of them defiantly, some hopelessly and despairingly. Old Tom clambers down from his post.)

ONE OR TWO OTHERS. We'll follow ye. We'll follow, Captain Borden!

BORDEN. Good. On Croatoan we'll start a new settlement.

OLD TOM *(With loud buoyancy.)* A new settlement!

ELEANOR. We'll begin there again.

RUNNER *(Fiercely.)* The Spaniards offer us food, I tell ye!

BORDEN *(Yelling.)* We'll never yield. We'll carry on the fight—on Croatoan—in the wilderness—wherever God sends us—and to the last man!

VOICES *(In a great husky groan.)* Food! The Spaniards will feed us.

OTHER VOICES. Food, food, give us food.

(Led by the runner, the group with him now moves swiftly and suddenly toward the left to go to the Spaniards. But Old Tom steps in front of them, lifting his musket menacingly.)

OLD TOM *(Yelling.)* Back, back! I'll kill the first man tries to pass me!
(He cuts at them with his musket. Before his bloodthirsty manner they hesitate.)

ELIZABETH GLANE. Then feed us!

(This sets the mutineers off again and they move forward. Old Tom fires his musket across in front of them. Two soldiers rush down from the colonists' houses at the rear with muskets and join Old Tom. The runner and his mutineers are stopped.)

BENNETT *(Yelling at them.)* And it would be the food of slaves!

(The youth who had gone off reappears with a huge white sheet held aloft on a halberd. The mutineers rally solidly around it and the runner.)

MUTINEERS. Surrender! Surrender!

(The youth waves the white cloth aloft, and the mutineers start off again to the left in a body. Led by Dame Colman, several of the women fling themselves on the youth and tear the white cloth from him.)

DAME COLMAN *(Fiercely as they overpower the youth.)* Use my one bed
sheet would ye, ye cowardly knave! *(She kicks at the now groveling youth and clutches her precious sheet to her.)* The times John Borden held your fevered hand and nursed ye back from death! *(She kicks at him again and then turns with fury on the mutineers.)* God in heaven witness me, ye shall all burn in hellfire if ye desert us now!

(The mutineers glare at her. Bennett lifts a flag from near the chapel and stands by Borden. Borden begins to speak with fervent earnestness.)

BORDEN. You shall know all and make your choice. True, the Spaniards
ask us to surrender. True, they will spare our lives, they will feed us.
(Lifting his hands high and continuing, his voice deepening with fervor.)
The question is clear—shall it be dishonor and life, or a brave struggle
onward— *(Gesturing off to the right.)* —out there—even to an end no
man knows.

OLD TOM. We'll fight!

A GROUP *(Led by the runner.)* No, no!

BORDEN. I know what it means to make this choice. And I know you will make it and you will not fail. You will stand firm for the colony.

(As Borden continues his pleading, some of the mutineers begin to move back from the runner's group to him and to the flag.)

JOYCE ARCHARD *(As she brings forward the citie's coat of arms and holds it up.)* Aye, aye, John Borden.

BORDEN *(With suddenly loud and crushing convincingness.)* As for me, I will die before I surrender. *(More loudly.)* Here in this new world we have planted the emblem of our race— *(With a gesture toward the flag held by Bennett.)* —of people who are free!

(A few more mutineers turn back toward Borden.)

DAME COLMAN AND OTHERS. And we'll be free!

(Father Martin enters waveringly from the rear.)

BORDEN. And in Sir Walter's name, and in the name of her who stands beside me— *(He reaches out and takes Eleanor's hand.)* —let us swear to be true to ourselves and the trust reposed in us.

SEVERAL VOICES *(A little stronger now.)* Yea, Captain Borden! God bless you! Bless you, Mistress Eleanor.

BORDEN *(With more certainty, a touch of exultation creeping into his voice.)* By the death of our friends and companions— *(He gently removes his hat and some of the men do likewise.)* —and those who lie buried in this ground, let us swear our consecration to the best that is in us.

OLD TOM AND ELEANOR. We swear!

JOYCE ARCHARD, DAME COLMAN AND OTHERS. We swear!

(More of the mutineers return to Borden's group.)

BORDEN *(His voice soaring through the night, his eyes straining ahead as if searching to see the invisible enemy hidden in the darkness which he challenges.)* Let the wilderness drive us forth as wanderers across the earth, scatter our broken bones upon these sands, it shall not kill the purpose that brought us here!

VOICES *(Still more strongly.)* No, John Borden. We will stand with ye, Captain Borden. Stand with ye.

(By this time the group around the runner has shrunk to some four or five people. But these are sullen and determined not to yield to Borden's persuasion.)

BORDEN. For it shall live. *(Loudly.)* Shall live!

(Bennett holds the flag triumphantly aloft. Joyce lifts the coat of arms likewise.)

VOICES. We're not afraid. Speak, lead us!

BORDEN. And down the centuries that wait ahead there'll be some whisper of our name, some mention and devotion to the dream that brought us here. And now into the hand of God we commend us. Amen.

OTHERS *(Fervently.)* Amen.

(Led by Borden and Eleanor, they all sweep forward a step or two and kneel. After an instant Borden rises and the others also rise.)

BORDEN. And now every man to his duty!

OLD TOM. On to Croatoan! *(He hurries out at the left.)*

BORDEN. Bennett, see to the supplies. *(He goes out at the right with Eleanor.)*

BENNETT. Aye, sir. *(Calling as he goes away at the left.)* Double load every musket!

VOICES. We will that, sir. Down with the Spaniards!

RUNNER. We will not go!

THE GROUP OF MUTINEERS. No! No!

(The colonists scatter in all directions. The runner and his little group move up into the shadows at the left rear. Reverend Martin creeps slowly to the chapel and kneels in front of it, bowing his head in a last silent prayer. The light fades down somewhat on the scene as the historian speaks.)

HISTORIAN *(From the shadows at the left.)* And so the colony made ready to leave the fort, driving themselves on with their last gasp of energy and strength. And even the rebellious ones shared in the tragedy of their going. In the cold hours before dawn they began their march into the vast unknown.

(The light fades from the historian and comes quickly in again on the center stage. The music strikes up the hymn with which the play opened, and the colonists weakly arrange themselves in marching order. Two soldiers with muskets lead the procession, followed by Bennett with the flag, and Joyce with the coat of arms, then Eleanor with Virginia Dare in her arms and Borden with her, and after them the men, women and children of the colony. Old Tom and Agona are at the end of the line. So the march begins toward the right and up along the edge of the woods. Old Tom calls out.)

OLD TOM. Sing, me hearties, sing. *(He leads off and the others join in.)*

COLONISTS.
   O God that madest heaven
   And hedged the seas around,
   Who that vast firmament on high
   With golden stars hath bound.

(As the people move on, the rebellious ones are pulled as if against their will into the march one by one. Father Martin feebly falls. The runner, the last of the rebelling group, hurries forward and lifts him up, and the two move on. The faces of the colonists are raised now, their forms beginning to be energized as they sing. Straight ahead they stare as if looking down the long road which

they must travel to the end. At the top of the rise in the edge of the woods Borden and Eleanor stop and turn, as the last of the procession passes by them. They stand looking back on the deserted fort. The light emphasizes them there and fades from the center stage. Another light comes on now, illuminating in a tight spot the flag flying gallantly from the rampart. The song has continued.)

O God, our mighty Father,
O bright immortal one,
Secure within thy mercy,
We walk this way alone.

(Borden swings his hand toward the fort in a final farewell. Then putting his arm around Eleanor as if to protect her from whatever lies ahead, he turns, and the two of them plunge into the darkness, following the others. The music continues as the light fades from the scene. The illumination holds on the flag. After an instant the music dies out, and now from the strangely luminous air high above the chapel the echo voices of the colonists are heard in the final words of the hymn, coming as it were from the very deep of heaven—"We walk this way alone." The light fades out.)

THE END

MEMBERS OF THE LOST COLONY

In all editions of *The Lost Colony* but one (1954) Paul Green began with a dedication page reading,

Then from colony records he listed members of the colony on Roanoke Island in 1587.

John White, *Governor*

Assistants to
the Governor
Roger Baily
Christopher Cooper
Ananias Dare
Dionysius Harvie
George Howe
James Platt
Roger Pratt
John Sampson
Thomas Stevens

Other Members
of the Colony
MEN
Maurice Allen
Arnold Archard
Richard Arthur
Mark Bennett
William Berde
Henry Berry
Richard Berry
Michael Bishop

John Borden
John Bridger
John Bright
John Brooke
Henry Browne
William Browne
John Burdon
Thomas Butler
Anthony Cage
John Chapman
John Cheven
William Clement
Thomas Colman
John Cotsmur
Richard Darige
Henry Dorrell
William Dutton
John Earnest
Thomas Ellis
Edmund English
John Farre
Charles Florrie
John Gibbes
Thomas Gramme
Thomas Harris (1)

Thomas Harris (2)
John Hemmington
Thomas Hewet
James Hynde
Henry Johnson
Nicholas Johnson
Griffin Jones
John Jones
Richard Kemme
James Lasie
Peter Little
Robert Little
William Lucas
George Martin
Michael Myllet
Henry Mylton
Humphrey Newton
William Nichols
Henry Paine
Hugh Pattenson
Thomas Phevens
Edward Powell
Henry Rufoote
Thomas Scot
Richard Shabedge

Thomas Smith
William Sole
John Spendlove
John Starte
John Stilman
Martin Sutton
Richard Taverner
Hugh Tayler
Clement Taylor
Richard Tomkins
Thomas Topan
John Tydway
Ambrose Viccars
Thomas Warner
William Waters
Cuthbert White
Richard Wildye
Robert Wilkinson
William Willes

Lewes Wotton
John Wright
Bryan Wyles
John Wyles

WOMEN

Joyce Archard
Alice Chapman
—— Colman
Eleanor Dare
Elizabeth Glane
Margery Harvie
Jane Jones
Margaret Lawrence
Jane Mannering
Emma Merimoth
Rose Payne
Jane Pierce
Winnifred Powell

Audry Tappan
Elizabeth Viccars
Joan Warren
Agnes Wood

CHILDREN

Thomas Archard
Virginia Dare
Robert Ellis
—— Harvie
George Howe, Jr.
Thomas Humfrey
John Pratt
John Sampson, Jr.
Thomas Smart
Ambrose Viccars
William Wythers

INTRODUCTION (DIALOGUE AT EVENING)
By Paul Green, from the 1946 Edition

CRITIC: *(As they stroll.)* This play must have been an undertaking. *(He gestures towards an outdoor theatre near by.)*
AUTHOR: It was.

"What with that huge stockade around the fort, and the blockhouse, the chapel, the cabins, the amphitheatre, the stage, the dressing rooms, and the water system, hot and cold. *(Gazing about him.)* It must have been a lot of work."

"It was, and a lot of folks did it."

"How many people would you say have been involved in the project?"

"Counting the workers, the actors, the technicians, and the citizens of the island, I should say about a thousand. Maybe more from first to last."

"Remarkable. It's a real community endeavor, isn't it?"

"Yes."

"But a little puzzling to find a venture like this down in a lonely country and so far from civilization."

"Hm-mm."

"Well, I mean so far from any big city. Norfolk is the nearest large town, isn't it?"

"Yes, about ninety miles away."

"That's what I thought. Where do your audiences come from?"

"They come from everywhere, like you and me."

"Yes, but I have a sort of professional reason for coming. I am a critic."

"The people come unprofessionally and because they want to see the show."

"Oh, yes. Of course. Do you plan to run it year after year?"

"Yes, that is the intent of those in charge. We will continue it as long as the public will support it. I hope it will be going fifty years from now."

"I hope your hopes will be realized but—" *(Staring off across the sound at the solitary Wright Memorial and the sand dunes in the distance.)* —"It's a lonely country all right. Look at that water there in the sound—motionless, smooth as glass. Life stands still."

"But sometimes it cuts up. . . . The sound I mean."

"You wouldn't think it. How do your New York actors like it here?"

"Most of them want to come back each year."

"And how do they get along with the natives?"

"The natives get along with them fine."

"What do the people do for a living here?"

"They farm, hunt, fish, do coast guard work—all sorts of things—and in the summer put on the play and take care of the people who come to see it."

"And now about the play itself. How did *The Lost Colony* come to be produced in the first place?"

"I hardly know. I suppose it was because the people on Roanoke Island wanted it and worked for it. For a long while they had held some sort of local celebration off and on each August 18th in honor of Virginia Dare's birthday."

"Virginia Dare?"

"In the school books it tells how she was the first child born of English parents in the New World."

"I remember now. It has been so long ago."

"Yes, we all forget. That's why plays are written, so we won't, don't you think?"

"Perhaps. And then?"

"Well, the island people took the initiative in the matter. Led by our local Mr. D. B. Fearing and aided by Mr. W. O. Saunders, an editor from Elizabeth City (that's a town up in the mainland) they all set about preparing plans for a 350th anniversary celebration to memorialize Sir Walter Raleigh's lost colony and Virginia Dare. One of the plans was to hold a nationwide beauty contest to select the girl who should play Virginia Dare. At that time they didn't know, nor did I, that when the play came to be written she would be a baby and remain so. In all our minds was the legend that she grew up to be a beautiful maiden, fell in love with the Indian chief Manteo's son, married him, and became the mother of a brave race that somehow evaporated into thin air. As Mr. Fearing, Mr. Saunders, and others went on with their work, I, who had always been interested in the romantic and tragic story of these early colonists, joined with them. But our combined efforts produced little more than pledges of money and cooperation, and with the deepening of the depression they amounted to little. Then came the WPA and saved us. Mr. Fearing and his helpers got a project approved to build the theatre, and I set about writing the play. With the aid of Congressman Lindsay Warren, 25,000 memorial fifty-cent coins were minted by the United States which were sold to collectors for a dollar and a half each. Through this means some funds were raised to pay the necessary proportion of materials for the project. And so we were started. But only started, for as the size of the production grew the need for more money increased. The night we opened we were deeply in debt. At least Mr. Fearing and certain local business men were."

"And the production paid out?"

"Yes."

"You were lucky."

"We all were. If it hadn't been for the WPA and the Federal Theatre—"

"Well, we can leave that out. You know how my paper feels about the New Deal and boondoggling. And now what do you consider to be the main factors in the success of the play?"

"The main reason was that our business manager and key man, Mr. D. B. Fearing, was a confirmed and energetic optimist. No sight of bad luck or fear of failure could stop him. Also another reason was that the local people were interested both as helpers and as active participants in the show. Then we had a fine and understanding director in Mr. Samuel Selden, a devoted builder in Mr. Albert Q. Bell, and a gifted newspaper man in Mr. Ben Dixon MacNeill, who throughout the first summer kept writing vivid human interest stories about the production. And finally, maybe the music, color, and movement of the play itself attracted the public. And those who came kept passing the word along to others. These were the main reasons, I suppose—not forgetting the technicians and actors, of course."

"I notice in the program here you call *The Lost Colony* a symphonic drama. Is it because you have music in it?"

"No, not primarily. I have used the phrase to describe one or two other plays I've written. It's not a perfect-fitting term but the best I can find, better than music or musical drama. In the original sense it means 'sounding together.' That is, all the elements of the theatre working together—music, song, dance, pantomime, etc."

"It's something new, isn't it?"

"No, it's pretty much as old as drama itself. The Greeks and the people of medieval and Elizabethan England produced outdoor plays like this.

And years ago Percy Mackaye wrote and produced masques and pageants somewhat like it."

"Do you call it a pageant or a play?"

"A play. For it tells a story, and the characters are individuals—at least I mean them to be—not types, as is usually the case in masques and pageants."

"Do you think the idea will spread and other localities will produce such plays?"

"I hope so. It seems to me there is a great chance for this kind of drama in America. This is a vast country full of legends and rich in story and song—all waiting to be used. And with the convenience of the automobile there is no reason why audiences cannot be drawn to any place if there's a colorful and interesting show to be seen. And there's something about a production outdoors that seems to fit the temper of the American people— maybe all people for that matter. Within the next few years I hope to see hundreds of summer dramatic festivals and productions scattered over the land from coast to coast. That would be one more way of making our people's lives vivid and more worth while. Then maybe we would begin to have a real people's theatre, other than the movies."

"I've heard a great deal of talk in my time about a people's theatre. What do you mean by it?"

"I mean a theatre in which plays are written, acted, and produced for and by the people—for their enjoyment and enrichment and not for any special monetary profit. Then when the country becomes theatre-minded, the level of taste and appreciation will gradually rise higher and higher. And some day the mountain peaks of drama—men like Aeschylus, Lope de Vega, and Shakespeare—may rise on the solid base beneath. As long as the American drama stays bottled up in the narrow neck and cul-de-sac of Broadway we can expect nothing better than what we have. I don't mean bottled up exactly, for already groups and sections of the country are turning their backs on the professional theatre and beginning to write and produce their own plays and the plays of others in a style equal to the best. For instance, the finest production of *The Cherry Orchard* I ever saw was at the University of Iowa some years ago."

"But surely you don't think the amateur theatre can measure up to the high standards of Broadway generally?"

"I don't know how high the standards of Broadway are generally, but the amateur theatre not only can measure up to them, but will, and more and more so as time goes on. The decentralization of the theatre has already set in."

"I don't share your enthusiasm there. Nothing bores me so much as an amateur play. Frankly that's why I'm not so sure I'm going to like *The Lost Colony*. From the list here it seems there are too many amateurs in it."

"They're not theatre people. Most of them have other jobs to do and they act for the pleasure in it. I think they're wise. When you consider the thousands of young people wearing out their fathers' shoe leather tramping the fruitless pavement of Broadway, and think of the fine things they might be doing back in their home neighborhood or town—"

"Frankly I think you are unfair to Broadway. You've never looked at it justly nor given it a real try. You ought to, you know, for your own sake as a writer."

"Oh, I hope to continue writing plays for Broadway now and then."

"But that's not the way to do it. You must throw yourself whole-heartedly into it."

"I've thought a lot about that, too."

"And what sort of answer did you arrive at?"

"This." *(With a gesture.)*

"Oh, well—" *(Looking at his watch.)* "It must be about time for the show to start."

"It is." *(He stares off at the wide western sky.)*

"Are you planning any other productions like this?" *(They turn.)*

"One I've thought about a great deal is to be in western North Carolina—that is, if we can find some business men up there willing to take the financial risk. I want to see the most beautiful outdoor theatre in the world built there on a mountain top close to the stars. And with the music, song, ballad, and dance of the people as material to work from, a beautiful and inspiring play can be done. Already I imagine great crowds of people coming from the south and from the north, moving along the skyline drive of the eastern world, all coming to see it. It's nothing but a dream, but some day—"

"Well, good luck. *(As a great diapason of sound suddenly breaks across the twilight.)* There, I hear the organ. Sounds rather nice."

"It sounds wonderful to me."

(They go up towards the amphitheatre.)

THE BEGINNING OF *The Lost Colony*
By Paul Green, from the 1954 Edition

I

Back in 1921 when I was a student at the University of North Carolina and trying to turn out one-act plays fast enough to equal the measure of Professor Frederick Koch's inspiration, I got to thinking about the story of Sir Walter Raleigh's tragic lost colony as subject matter for a play. So I decided to go down to Roanoke Island on the coast and look around at the original site of the colonization attempt. I set out from Chapel Hill and traveled by bus and train to Beaufort, thence up Pamlico Sound by mailboat, and finally made the latter part of my journey across the open inlet by hiring a fisherman and his little motorboat—in all a distance of some three hundred miles. I still remember that fisherman, a muscular old fellow, sturdy and craggy and coming back to me now in visualization like that old man Ernest Hemingway wrote about recently in his great sea story. He sang a song to me as we went across. I still can remember some of the words—

> "Oh, haul away, bully boys,
>   Oh, haul away high-o
> We'll wipe away the morning dew
>   And then go below."

It was night when I arrived at the little town of Manteo. I got a room at a local boarding house and early the next morning started walking up the sandy road through the forest toward the place known as Fort Raleigh four miles away. I plodded along in the ankle-deep sand, and the sun was coming up in its great holocaust of flame when I got to the little grove of pines and live oaks on the edge of Croatan Sound and stood beside the small squat stone erected in 1896 to Virginia Dare, the first English child born in the new world. I wandered around in the woods. I idly plucked some sassafras twigs and chewed them, and thought upon that band of hardy pioneers who, three hundred and thirty-four years before, had come to this spot to build a fort, a bastion, a beachhead for the extension of the English-speaking empire across the sea. In a hollytree a mocking bird trilled a time-less note.

I thought of the hardships that these people had suffered, of the dark nights, the loneliness, the despair and frustration here, desolate and forgot by Queen Elizabeth in her concern with her Spanish war in England far away. In my mind I could hear the cries of the sick and hungry little chil-dren, see the mothers bending above their rough home-made cribs as they twisted and turned in their fever and their fret. And what anguish, what heartache and homesickness! And ever the anxious expectant look toward the eastern sea where never the bright sail of a ship was seen nor the mari-ner's cheer was heard to tell that help was nigh. Night after night, day after day, only the murmur of the vast and sheeted waters, only the sad whisper-ing of the dark forest to break upon their uneasy dreams.

Yes, here on the very spot where I stood all this had happened, all this had been endured.

II

I came away charged with inspiration to write a drama on the lost colony. Back in Chapel Hill I promised "Proff," as we all affectionately called Pro-fessor Koch, to have a piece for his play-writing class come the next week. I turned out a one-acter for production in the University Forest Theatre. It told an imaginary story of Virginia Dare and how she grew up and lived in the wilderness among the Indians, falling in love with Chief Manteo's son and marrying him—a forest idyll. But the class didn't think much of it. Proff Koch didn't care for it either, though he smiled and said it had good points. By that time I thought it was pretty rotten. Somewhere along the line my inspiration had petered out. I had come home and started reading too much in the literature of the subject, I guess. One piece that had stuck in my mind was a long poem by a North Carolina author which told the made-up legend of how Virginia Dare, as a beautiful young woman, had been turned into a white doe by the spell of an angry Indian suitor and how she had been mistakenly shot by the arrow of her own true lover, another Indian brave—only returning to her beautiful maidenly self in the throes of death.

So I threw the play away, and turned back to writing furiously about the poor whites and the Negroes of my native county in Eastern North Carolina.

III

Ten years later I was teaching philosophy in the University of North Carolina. One day there came a knock on my office door and W. O. Saunders, of Elizabeth City, North Carolina, entered. Saunders was the editor of an active paper in his town, known as the *Independent*. At that time he was famous locally not for his editorship of a liberal and outspoken paper or as a contributor of articles to *Collier's Magazine*, but for his recent pioneer activity of walking up and down Broadway in New York City in the mid-heat of summer, wearing pajamas and carrying a sign advocating a change to sensible summer clothing for the comfort of the American male.

Saunders explained to me that he had been in Germany some months past and had seen the great Bavarian outdoor religious play at Oberammergau.

"Paul," he said, "we've got to have something like that in North Carolina. And I've got an idea."

Then he went on to say that the story of Sir Walter Raleigh's lost colony, he thought, would make a good drama. "I hear you've already written something about it," he said. I told him I had tried a piece on Virginia Dare, but it hadn't worked out.

"You see," he said, "1937 will soon be here. This will mark the 350th anniversary of the colony and the birth of Virginia Dare also. We ought to have a great exposition—something like the Jamestown Exposition of 1907. We could move a tribe of Indians down on Roanoke Island, let them carry on farming, raise tobacco, set their fishing weirs, just the way they did at the time Sir Walter sent his colony over. We could have every man on the island grow a beard and the people could wear the dress of three centuries ago." He got excited, his eyes shone. "It would be the biggest thing ever to hit North Carolina," he said. "We would get nationwide, even worldwide publicity for it."

We talked some more and finally agreed to have a meeting down in the little town of Manteo on Roanoke Island. The date was set for three weeks later, and my wife and I drove down there overland, and in the courthouse the project of doing a drama was initiated. The idea of a full-blown exposition seemed by this time to be too ambitious an undertaking. Also we were realizing that the Carolina fishermen wouldn't take to the idea of growing beards and wearing doublet and hose.

W. O. Saunders made a speech that night. I made a talk, but the crowded courthouse still seemed rather cold and unenthusiastic. Suddenly from the back of the hall a bell-like voice rang out, the voice of United States Senator Josiah William Bailey. He and Lindsay Warren, who was then a Congressman and later became Comptroller General of the United States, were down at nearby Nags Head on a fishing expedition. They had come over to the courthouse meeting and sat in the back unrecognized. Now Senator Bailey got up, strode down the aisle and delivered a speech that soon had everybody eager for activity. He made it quite clear to us that Roanoke Island was the true inspiration for Shakespeare's play, *The Tempest*. And then he quoted several parts of the play in a voice that sent the chills running up and down our backs.

"When Shakespeare wrote 'Come unto these yellow sands,'" he said, "he had in mind the sands of Roanoke Island. No doubt about it. The tragedy of the lost colony that happened on this island inspired the pen of the immortal Shakespeare to write one of his finest and most imaginative plays. This is a sacred spot here. Let us put on a drama, our drama, here at this patriotic shrine where those brave pioneers lived, struggled, suffered and died. Yes, let us tell their story to the world."

IV

After this, committees were set up, meetings held, and the Roanoke Island Historical Association was reactivated.

One of the meetings I especially remember. It was in Raleigh, and the Governor and a number of legislators were present. The newly-appointed promotion man arrived with a Hollywood-looking secretary on each arm and a big scrolled map drawn up which he exhibited triumphantly showing the whole of Roanoke Island's thousands of acres of land cut up in lots all numbered and ready for sale. We had to get rid of him.

And I felt the old feeling of that early summer morning ten years before coming back to me. A group of North Carolina and Norfolk, Virginia, businessmen agreed to raise the necessary funds for building the amphitheatre and producing the play. I got busy writing it.

This time let me hold true to the stimulation of my subject matter. Let me keep ever before me the sense and image of this group of tragic suffering people—more than a hundred and twenty of them—men, women and children who had fared forth from England on that fatal day in 1587 to brave the turmoil and terror of the vast and raging sea in search of their destiny, these the keepers of a dream. Away with all secondhand sources—let it come prime, let it come raw.

And I would forget the baby Virginia Dare except as one of the items in the whole dramatic symphony. Don't worry because the father's name Ananias must cause a dramatic emphasis different from that of history.

These didn't matter. The main thing was the people. For these were the folk of England, the folk of our race—these who now must labor with their hands to wrest from cryptic nature her goods and stores of sustenance, or die, these who now must live with their feet in the earth and their heads bare to the storms, the wind and sleet and the falling fire from heaven. Flood and drought and hunger are to be their lot, their minds and spirits a prey to the nightmare fear and horror of the dark and impenetrable wilderness around them.

And yet out of this testing, this straining and tension here on these lonely shores, this being hammered on an anvil of God, there must emerge the faith that lies native in them as workers, as believers, as spiritual beings who lift their eyes in awe to the great Presence riding the lightning flashes down the sky, the Power that breathes in earthquakes and the bellowing of the storm or sweetly sings His pleasure in the birds of spring and smiles His joy in the flowers by the road. Yea, out of this play must come a sustaining faith, their faith, a purified statement of aim and intent, of human purpose, or then all was waste and sacrifice made vain.

And so here on these yellow muted sands of Roanoke Island, let my hero, John Borden Everyman, speak out in the play on the night he and his companions are to disappear into the vast unknown out of our sight forever— let him speak the words which are his credo and our credo as self-reliant and valiant men—"Hear that once Sir Walter said, the victory lieth in the struggle, not the city won. To all free men it standeth so, he said. And by the death of our friends and companions and those who lie buried in this ground, let us swear our consecration to the best that is in us. Let the wilderness drive us forth as wanderers across the earth, scatter our broken bones upon these sands, it shall not kill the purpose that brought us here! And down the centuries that wait ahead there'll be some whisper of our name, some mention and devotion to the dream that brought us here."

And let there be music, always music on which the story might ride.

V

Thus I struggled with the drama, trying to make it say something worthy of the lost and perished people about whom it was written.

Then as the months went by, the economic depression settled on down in its deadening freeze of the nation's sap and vitality. By this time hundreds of pledges had been made, amounting to a total, I was told, of some two hundred thousand dollars. But not one cent was ever collected from these sources. Still, W. O. Saunders and his associate, D. B. Fearing of Manteo, kept working, riding, talking, promoting the idea of the drama, and even going to Washington to confer more than once with Senator Bailey, Congressman Warren and others.

Finally, the agencies of the wpa, the cc Camp, and the Federal Theatre came into being. Through them and with the cooperation of the North Carolina Historical Association, the Roanoke Island Historical Association and the Carolina Playmakers our project at last was realized.

And with Samuel Selden as director and Frederick H. Koch as advisory director, the play opened for its first annual summer run on the night of July 4, 1937.